POPULATION SINCE THE INDUSTRIAL REVOLUTION

N. L. TRANTER

POPULATION SINCE THE INDUSTRIAL REVOLUTION

The Case of England and Wales

CROOM HELM LONDON

FIRST PUBLISHED 1973
© 1973 BY NEIL TRANTER

CROOM HELM LTD
2–10 ST JOHNS ROAD, LONDON SW11

HARDBACK ISBN 0–85664–012–3
PAPERBACK ISBN 0–85664–044–1

PRINTED IN GREAT BRITAIN
BY EBENEZER BAYLIS AND SON LTD
THE TRINITY PRESS, WORCESTER, AND LONDON
BOUND BY G. & J. KITCAT LTD, LONDON

Contents

To my Mother and Father

Acknowledgements

I would like to record my gratitude to the following authors and publishers for allowing me to reproduce certain extracts from their work:

Penguin Books Ltd. and E. M. Hubback, *The Population of Britain*, London, 1947;

The Bodley Head Ltd. and A. Marwick, *Britain in the Century of Total War*, London, 1968, Pelican Books, 1970;

George Weidenfeld & Nicolson and E. A. Wrigley, *Population and History*, London, 1969;

Cambridge University Press and G. T. Griffith, *Population Problems in the Age of Malthus*, Cambridge, 1926;

Martin Seckar & Warburg Ltd. and R. and K. Titmuss, *Parents' Revolt*, London, 1942;

The Clarendon Press and J. D. Chambers, *Population, Economy and Society in Pre-industrial England*, Oxford, 1972 (edited by W. A. Armstrong);

Population Studies and S. Cherry, 'The role of a provincial hospital: the Norfolk and Norwich hospital, 1771–1880', *Population Studies*, XXVI, 2, 1972, pp. 291–306;

Jonathan Cape Ltd. and H. Cox, *The Problem of Population*, London, 1922;

The Royal Statistical Society and E. C. Snow, 'The limits of industrial employment (II): The influence of the growth of population on the development of industry', *Journal of the Royal Statistical Society*, XCVIII, Pt. II, 1935, pp. 239–73;

The Sources of History Ltd., Hodder and Stoughton Ltd. and T. H. Hollingsworth, *Historical Demography*, London, 1969;

The Controller of Her Majesty's Stationery Office, Royal Commission on Population *Report*, Cmd. 7695, 1949; and *Cardington Census Enumerators' Books*, 1851, HO 107/1752, 3955.

I would also like to express my sincere thanks to those of my colleagues and former colleagues who gave freely of their time and energy to discuss the problems of English population with me: among them Mr S. Cherry, Dr T. R. Gourvish, Mr J. R. Hay and Mr M. Miller. They are, however, in no way responsible for the inadequacies which remain in the volume. I owe a very special debt to the late David Chambers, Emeritus Professor of Economic and Social History at the University of Nottingham, not only for first arousing my interest in demographic questions but also for giving me the opportunity to pursue it. I regret that I know of no form of words with which to do adequate justice to the help, stimulation and kindliness that I received from him.

Lastly, my thanks are due to Miss Margaret Hendry of the University of Stirling for typing the manuscript so speedily and so efficiently despite the many other calls on her time.

Introduction

This book is intended to serve as a brief introduction to the study of the population of England and Wales since the early eighteenth century. It aims to describe the pattern of population growth, and to examine some of its principal causes and consequences. In writing it I have been conscious of several major problems.

Not least of these is the need to justify the appearance of yet another book on English historical demography. There are, after all, already a number of excellent introductory texts on the subject, and at one stage I seriously doubted whether there was any room for another.* In the end, however, I decided that there was.

My decision was based on two considerations. The first was a personal belief that the subject of English historical demography is broad enough and fascinating enough to bear the weight of many more books yet. Dr Hollingsworth has recently reminded us of the importance of the population factor in history:

> . . . with a better knowledge of population movements, a good deal of history can be seen as drifting down a stream, most of the leading events fitting into the demographically determined pattern. . . . In a sense, population can thus be used to explain history, as worthy of effort as memorizing dates of kings or battles. . . . One may, indeed, trace trends in the very civilization and culture of mankind from the population figures, and conversely one may try to build up a population history from knowledge of the conditions of society (T. H. Hollingsworth, *Historical Demography*, London, 1969).

---

*Among them E. A. Wrigley, *Population and History*, London, 1969; M. W. Flinn, *British Population Growth, 1700–1850*, London, 1970; H. J. Habakkuk, *Population Growth and Economic Development since 1750*, Leicester University Press, 1971; J. D. Chambers, *Population, Economy and Society in Pre-industrial England*, Oxford University Press, 1972.

Although this is undoubtedly something of an exaggeration, I
share sufficient of Dr Hollingsworth's belief in the significance
of the population variable in history to believe that the danger of
diminishing returns arising from too many books on the population question is still a long way off.

The second and more practical consideration which persuaded
me to continue was the belief that one of the greatest problems
confronting anyone coming fresh to the study of English population history is the vast array of literature with which he must
grapple—a literature that is scattered over a wide range of books,
monographs and periodicals, not all of them easily accessible nor
at first sight seemingly relevant. My main purpose, therefore, has
been to attempt to draw together and summarise as much of this
material as possible in one reasonably short volume. In doing so
I have, unavoidably, often given vent to my own personally
held opinions both on the strengths and weaknesses of the available demographic data, and on the causes and consequences of
demographic trends. But I would not like to think that this was
achieved at the expense of the general synthesis for which I was
primarily aiming.

The second problem of which I have been conscious in writing
this book is essentially one of emphasis and method of approach.
Some time ago Professor Lewis wrote that 'there is no single
theory of economic growth. The factors which determine growth
are numerous, and each has its own set of theories' and 'the
various causes of growth cannot be separated except for analytic
purposes' (W. A. Lewis, *The Theory of Economic Growth*, London,
1955). These are views which I share unreservedly. Population
is only one of the many variables which together determine the
pace and character of economic and social development. It may,
arguably, be one of the most important. But population alone is
not the engine of economic and social progress. Nor are demographic consequences the only consequences of economic and
social change that are worth considering. I stress this here because
in isolating one variable for special treatment, as this book does,
one runs the very grave risk of overstating its relative importance.
If in what follows I have fallen into this trap I can only say that
I had absolutely no wish to do so. Readers will also note that, like
Professor Lewis, the approach I have adopted is a highly artificial

one. I have separated my analysis of the causes and consequences
of population change in a way that bears no comparison with the
real world. I have done so merely to simplify the complexities
involved. In reality, of course, the relationship between population, economy and society is so intricate and so intertwined that
it defies separation.

A third problem of which I have been all too well aware is
that of personal inadequacy in trying to cope with the task I have
set myself. The attraction and certainly the challenge of historical
demography is that it encompasses a bewilderingly wide variety of
academic disciplines—economics, sociology, palaeography, history, and many, many more. To do full justice to a study of the
evolution, causes and consequences of population change one
needs to be able to command a range of talents so broad that it
almost defies listing, and so varied that it far exceeds the competence of any one single person. Personally, I can claim a partial
competence in only one or two of the required skills, and can
only hope that this does not mar what follows too seriously.

As if all this were not enough I would ask the reader to bear
one last point in mind. At present our knowledge of English
population history since the eighteenth century is still very far
from complete. Few firm conclusions can be drawn with any real
degree of confidence. Hopefully, this state of affairs will change
over the next few years when the results of the new techniques
of research pioneered at Cambridge and elsewhere become available. In the meantime, we are forced to recognise that much
remains unanswered, and that some at least of the conclusions
which now seem firm enough may themselves have to be modified
when we become better informed. Perhaps, therefore, this book
may best be regarded as an *interim* summary report.

1. *Sources and Methods*

There is no original or exciting way in which to begin a book about English population. Tedious though it undoubtedly is, our first task must be to assess the range and reliability of the various population statistics upon which our discussion is to be based. The reasons for this lie partly in the very complexity of the relationship between population, economy and society, and partly in the nature of the available population data themselves.

The association between population and economic and social development is a highly intricate one. Consider, for example, the influence exerted by the population variable on the pattern of economic growth. To a considerable extent the structure and progress of any economic unit is determined by its demographic characteristics. Unquestionably the sheer size of a population and the rate at which it is growing are the most important demographic determinants of economic development. But it would be very wrong to assume that they are the only ones. Thus the economic consequences of population growth in two populations which are growing at the same rate will vary according to whether growth has been due to changes in the rate of natural increase (i.e. in the amount by which the number of births exceeds the number of deaths) or to changes in the balance between in- and out-migration. In populations that are expanding by natural increase alone the economic effects of population growth will likewise be very different if the rising surplus of births over deaths has been caused by an increase in fertility or a decrease in mortality. Again, populations of the same size, which are growing at the same rate, may be at altogether different stages of economic development according to the influence exercised by their respective age, sex and marital structures. The point is that a thorough appreciation of the way in which the population variable affects the performance of an economy requires the provision of an elaborate range of demographic data: on variations in the pace of natural increase and in the balance of in- and out-migration; on trends in the levels of fertility and mortality; on age, sex and marital composition; as well as on population size and rates of growth. Clearly, it is imperative that we test the ability of our source-materials and methods of procedure to yield information of such scope, if only to understand at the outset what the possible limitations of our analysis are going to be.

There is, however, a much more urgent reason for beginning with a close look at the nature of the relevant statistics. For much of the period with which we are concerned, until that is well into the nineteenth century, the range of sources capable of providing detailed and reliable population data is known to be extremely limited. Moreover, until very recently, the techniques which have normally been relied upon to extract information from such sources have, it must be admitted, been rather crude. Unfortunately, some of the earliest studies of English population history were far too indiscriminate in the source-materials they chose to use, and far too uncritical of the analytical techniques they adopted. As a result the relatively few accurate population statistics which can be provided for the eighteenth and early nineteenth centuries have often been submerged in a welter of much less satisfactory data. Not surprisingly, anyone coming fresh to the study of historical demography is likely to become rapidly confused by what he finds. The only way to ease his dilemma is to spend some time considering the adequacy of each of the main source-materials and methods of analysis upon which the available demographic data have been based. Perhaps then the newcomer will be better able to separate the material which is worth using from that which is not.

In the last few years the need to look first at the range and reliability of our statistical information has been given fresh impetus by the notable advances which have been made in the techniques of historical demographic research, and by the claims made for them. According to their originators the application of 'family reconstitution' procedures to the material contained in the parish registers of the Anglican church, the processing of data contained in so-called 'listings of inhabitants', and the intensive use of nineteenth-century census enumerators' books will ultimately supply the necessary harvest of detailed and accurate population statistics which demographic historians require. The results of the pioneer researches based on such 'new' sources and

techniques are already available to us, and many more are in the
pipe-line. No doubt they will help to fill in a number of the
present gaps in our knowledge. But will they prove to be quite so
fruitful as their supporters claim? Will they solve *all* the major
problems confronting those of us interested in charting the
history of English population, particularly during the period
before the middle of the nineteenth century? As we shall see there
are grounds for believing that they will not. The danger is that
in our desperation for any crumbs of statistical comfort we might
accept the findings of the 'new' historical demography without
paying sufficient attention to their undoubted weaknesses and
limitations. This is a temptation that must be resisted, even if it
means devoting a substantial introductory section to an admittedly
unexciting discussion of source-materials and methodology.

* * *

The most convenient place to begin is in the nineteenth century
when both the quantity and quality of population data improve
rapidly. As the science of economic theory became more sophisticated, society grew increasingly aware of the significance of the
part played by population change in economic, social and political
development, and for the first time the State began to take a keen
and sustained interest in the provision of reliable population
statistics. Those nonsensical eighteenth-century notions that the
collection and publication of population data by the State was an
infringement of personal liberty, a mischievous device for im-
posing additional taxation, or a threat to national security gradually disappeared. From the nineteenth century onwards the range
and depth of easily available demographic data expanded steadily.
Perhaps the most important turning-points occurred in 1801
with the introduction of the decennial civil census, in 1841 when
the methods of census-taking were greatly improved, and in 1837
when the Registrar-General's returns of births, marriages and
deaths first began.

The first official census of England and Wales was taken in
1801, and others followed at regular ten-yearly intervals until
1941 when the pattern was temporarily broken by the exigencies
of the Second World War. Before that of 1841, the collection of
census information was left in the hands of largely unsupervised

enumerators, usually local poor-law overseers, who visited each household in their parish and entered the results of their inquiries on specially devised tally-sheets. Few of the original tally-sheets now survive. In any case, reliance on ill-educated and often carelessly chosen enumerators working without close supervision, and on tally-sheet procedures was not likely to produce particularly reliable or particularly detailed results. 'Door-step' answers are often notoriously inaccurate, and the range of questions which can be asked of the householder under such conditions is necessarily limited. Consequently the early census inquiries provide information to varying degrees of accuracy on the size and sex structure of the population, on the number of households and families it contained, and (from 1821) on its age-structure—but little else that is of much use to the demographer.

In 1841, however, the procedures of census-taking changed for the better. The recently appointed registrars of births, marriages and deaths were given the additional responsibility of supervising the periodic collection of census data in their own Registration Districts, and much greater care was taken in the selection of local enumerators. At the same time, in place of the existing tally-sheet methods, each householder was to receive in advance a separate census schedule which, in theory anyway, he was required to fill in personally before returning to his local enumerator. These individual schedules were then laboriously, and on the whole carefully, copied into 'enumerators' books' upon which the official census publications were ultimately based. Despite the many *potential* sources of error, the fact remains that the new techniques brought an immediate improvement in the reliability and sophistication of the census returns. The census of 1841, for example, asked each householder to record the name, age, sex, occupation and place of birth (whether elsewhere in England and Wales, in Scotland, Ireland or Foreign Parts) of every member of his household. That of 1851 went even further, asking for more precise information on place of birth (by parish and county), on the relationship of each individual to the household head, and on the marital status of every member of the household. Since 1851, further modifications and improvements have occasionally been made to census procedures. The census of 1911, for instance, included a detailed investigation into secular changes in the levels of marital fertility. That of 1921 asked for the

No. of Householder's schedule	Parish or Township of Cardington		Ecclesiastical District of	City or Borough of		Town of		Village of		
	Name of street, Place or Road, and Name or No. of House	Name and Surname of each Person who abode in the house on the Night of the 30th March, 1851.	Relation to Head of Family	Condition	Age of Males	Females	Rank, profession or Occupation	Where born	whether Blind or Deaf and Dumb		
3	Manor Farm	William Preston	Head	Mar	50		Farmer of 250 acres employs 7 labourers	Beds Cardington	
		Sarah ,,	Wife	Mar		44	Farmer's wife	Beds Bedford	
		Sarah ,,	Dau	U		19		,, Cottonend	
		Susannah Fitzhugh	Dau-in-law	U		18		,, Bedford	
		Jane Preston	Dau	U		15		,, Cottonend	
		Catherine Preston	Dau			11		,, ,,	
		Martha ,,	Dau			4		,, ,,	
		Emma ,,	Dau			3		,, ,,	
		William Parrott	Servant	U	23		Farm labourer	,, Cottonend	
4	Pastures	Samuel Preston	Head	M	54		Farmer 148 acres employing 9 labourers	Beds Cardington	
		Edee ,,	Wife	M		56	Farmer's wife	,, ,,	
		Caroline ,,	Dau	U		27		,, ,,	
		William ,,	Son	U	19			,, ,,	
		Harriett ,,	Dau	U		29		,, ,,	
		Richard Geary	Servant	U	12		Farm labourer	,, ,,	
5		Jacob Brabrooks	Head	Mar	47		Pig dealer	Bucks Newport	
		Mary ,,	Wife	Mar		38	Pig dealer's wife	Beds Cardington	
		George Brabrooks	Son	U	18		Pig dealer	,, ,,	
		James Brabrooks	Son	U	15		Servant	,, ,,	

Extract from Cardington, Beds., census enumerator's book, 1851.

whereabouts of all living children or step-children under the age of sixteen for each married or widowed adult. That of 1931 required details on the place of usual residence as well as on place of birth.

Without cataloguing all the alterations and additions that have been made to census inquiries since 1841, it is sufficient to note that from the middle of the nineteenth century the decennial census data gradually came to meet most of the requirements which an historical demographer could reasonably expect. They provide material on chronological and regional variations in the size and rate of growth of population, from 1801; on sex structures, from 1801; on age composition, from 1821 (except for a gap in 1831); on the frequency and direction of geographic mobility, from 1841; on marital structures, from 1851; on household and family size, from 1801, and on the detailed composition of households and families, from 1841 when the census enumerators' books first became available.

The second major turning-point in the evolution of population statistics during the nineteenth century came with the introduction of civil registration in 1837. From then onwards all births, marriages and deaths were to be reported to specially created district registrars who in turn submitted the details at quarterly intervals to the General Register Office at Somerset House. There the data were collated and published in the form of quarterly, annual, and in some cases weekly, reports. Legal penalties for the failure to notify a birth, marriage or death were not introduced until 1874, and partly because of this the registration of births remained incomplete until the early 1880s. On the whole, however, the registration of marriages and deaths has always been fairly accurate.

Civil registration provides historical demographers with the necessary raw materials for studying variations in the rate of natural increase and in the crude rates of birth, marriage and death both over time and between one geographic area and another. It allows a good deal more besides. The birth certificate which had to be completed by the parents required information on the sex of the child, the name and surname, rank or profession of the father, and the name and maiden surname of the mother. The certificate of death asked for details about the age, sex, rank or profession of the deceased, as well as about cause of death. That of marriage included questions on the age, marital status, ranks or professions of both parties, and on the occupations of their respective fathers. Much of the additional demographic data which can be gleaned from these certificates (on, for example, sex ratios at birth, cause of death by age, sex and profession, age at marriage by occupational status, marital status at time of marriage, illegitimacy rates, etc.) has already been compiled and tabulated by the General Register Office and is easily accessible in the annual reports of the Registrar-General. But a great deal more could be extracted if historical demographers were allowed unrestricted access to the individual certificates themselves.

By far the least satisfactory of all population statistics for the nineteenth and twentieth centuries are those relating to the movement of people into and out of England and Wales. Even so the data on international migration which are available from the second half of the nineteenth century are considerably better than any which exist for earlier periods, and they do improve in the course of time. The fullest analysis of overseas migration during the latter part of our period, that by Professor Brinley Thomas (*Migration and Economic Growth*), relies principally on the figures contained in shipboard passenger lists.

Registration District _____

1. _____.   BIRTH in the Sub-district of _____ in the _____

Columns :-	1	2	3	4	5	6	7	8	9	10
No.	When and where born	Name, if any	Sex	Name and surname of father	Name, surname and maiden-surname of mother	Occupation of father	Signature, description and residence of informant	When registered	Signature of registrar	Name entered after registration

Registration District _____

1. _____.   DEATH in the Sub-district of _____ in the _____

Columns :-	1	2	3	4	5	6	7	8	9
No :	When and where died	Name and surname	Sex	Age	Occupation	Cause of death	Signature, description and residence of informant	When registered	Signature of Registrar

Registration District of _____

19 _____.   Marriage solemnized at _____ in the
District of _____ in the _____

Columns :-	1	2	3	4	5	6	7	8
No :	When married	Name and surname	Age	Condition	Rank or profession	Residence at the time of marriage	Fathers name and surname	Rank or profession of father

Married in the _____ by _____ by me,

This marriage was solemnized between us { _____ } in the presence of us { _____ }

It should be stressed that the passenger lists include only those people who were travelling between the United Kingdom and countries outside Europe. They do not, therefore, provide any guide to changes in the balance of movement between Britain and Europe. Furthermore, only from 1912 were such passengers asked to declare whether or not they intended to alter their place of permanent residence. Though no doubt the overwhelming majority of people travelling between Britain and extra-European countries were genuine migrants, some were not. Before 1815 passenger returns are extant only for the brief period between December 1773 and April 1776, and simply record the total weekly number of people leaving the United Kingdom. They were suspended during the American War of Independence, and do not appear to have been resumed for some time thereafter. An Act of 1803, passed to help enforce official regulations governing the number of passengers per ship-ton, once again ordered the masters of all vessels leaving British ports to submit lists of their passengers. But no list survives before 1815, when the regular annual series at last begins. Not until 1853 were masters required to state the nationality of out-going passengers. Data on the number of people coming into the United Kingdom from countries outside Europe do not become available until 1855, and their various nationalities were not distinguished until as late as 1876. In short, the net balance of passenger movements can only be calculated with any degree of accuracy after 1855, and that of British citizens alone only after 1876.

Although passenger lists give a crude indication of variations in the rate of in- and out-migration and in the age, sex and occupational composition of migrants from the second half of the nineteenth century, in view of their obvious limitations it is fortunate that other sources are also available. Some idea of the numbers and proportions of Irishmen, Scotsmen and Persons of Other Nationalities can be obtained from the decennial census returns from 1841—statistics which are summarised in certain of the Registrar-Generals' reports. For the period after 1920 published data on the number of work-permits issued to aliens can be used for a similar purpose. But the simplest and most common method of measuring variations in the balance between in- and out-migration is to contrast the excess of births over deaths (derived from civil registration data) with the actual increase in population between two census dates. This technique has been followed in Chapter II below. It is, of course, possible only after 1841 when both census and civil registration returns are available.

Whatever its deficiencies, the fact remains that from about the middle of the nineteenth century the range of reliable and detailed population data which becomes available is quite adequate for most demographic needs. The greatest problem confronting population historians of this later period is how best to 'dig out, shape, and build up in an intelligent manner the figures which official publications provide in abundance' (T. A. Welton). There are problems enough in this, but they are relatively minor when contrasted with the difficulties faced by those of us interested in the demographic history of the eighteenth and early nineteenth centuries. In the absence of official population statistics, historical demographers of the period before the late 1830s and early 1840s face the additional task of having to compile their own series of population data. They must find source-materials which can be made to yield information on the size and rate of growth of the population, its age, sex and marital structures, its patterns of natural increase, fertility, mortality and migration habits. They must also devise techniques to test for the reliability of this information. We cannot even begin to discuss the causes and consequences of population trends during the period of early industrialisation without satisfying ourselves that historians have been, or are likely to be, successful in overcoming these additional challenges. Accordingly, the remainder, and of necessity the bulk, of this chapter must try to assess the adequacy of the various source-materials and methods of analysis upon which our eighteenth- and early nineteenth-century population statistics depend. In order to do this as simply as possible we will look separately at the sources and techniques normally used to provide data on firstly the size and rate of growth of the population, secondly natural increase and migration, and finally the trends in nuptiality, fertility and mortality rates. Discussion of the sources of information available for an analysis of age, sex and marital structures before census enumerators' books became available will be reserved until Chapter VI.

1. Population: Size and Rate of Growth

Before the introduction of the decennial census in 1801, all estimates of total population size, and thus of rates of population growth, must be compiled either from parish register returns of baptisms, marriages and burials, or from information contained in surviving 'listings of inhabitants'.

Those based on parish register data follow one of two procedures. By the first, the size of a population is derived from a simple division of the total number of baptisms, marriages or burials in a particular period by the assumed level of the crude baptism, marriage or burial rates per thousand population. For example, if 105 baptisms were recorded by the registers in the year 1750, and the level of the crude baptism rate for that year was assumed to be 35 per thousand population, then the total population in 1750 would be $105 \times \frac{1000}{35}$ i.e. 3,000. Alternatively, we can follow the technique known as 'counting-backwards'. Given a reliable estimate of total population in say 1801 (from the census), and given also that we know the annual number of baptisms (births) and burials (deaths) recorded in that population group before 1801 (from the parish registers), we can calculate the size of the population in a previous year, say 1791, simply by subtracting the total surplus of births over deaths in the period 1791–1801 from the 1801 figure. Thus 1,000 (the total population in 1801) minus 100 (the surplus of births over deaths between 1791 and 1801) = 900 (the estimated population in 1791).

Quite apart from the failings of the parish registers themselves, to which we shall return below, both of these techniques leave much to be desired. The reliability of the first largely depends on the accuracy of our assumptions regarding the levels of the vital rates of birth, marriage and death. Unfortunately these have never been precisely determined for the period before the 1840s. Birth-, death- and marriage-rates varied considerably from time to time and from one area to another. To assume as many have done that they remained constant and uniform throughout the entire period or that they were as high during the eighteenth century as they were to be in the late 1830s and 1840s (when the level of the vital rates can be calculated from census and civil registration data) is extremely unwise, and might lead to severe distortions in our estimates of total population. The second procedure, that of 'counting-backwards', makes no allowance for the effects of migration on the size and rate of growth of a population group. Among populations where the degree of in- and out-migration was negligible or evenly balanced this would not matter much. As has frequently been pointed out, however, the amount of popular spatial movement in eighteenth-century England was quite startling. Few areas, even in the remotest rural parts, remained untouched by the ebb and flow of internal migration. It follows from this that population estimates based on 'counting-backwards' techniques might easily be invalidated by the constantly changing patterns of internal geographic mobility.

Anglican church registers for the eighteenth and early nineteenth centuries are no longer extant for every parish in England and Wales. All estimates of national or county population size before 1801 depend entirely on the Abstract of Parish Register Returns compiled by John Rickman in the early nineteenth century. As part of his early census inquiries Rickman asked the keepers of the church registers in each parish to report the number of baptisms and burials recorded in their registers for every tenth year from 1700 to 1780 (1700–01, 1710–11, 1720–21 etc.) and annually thereafter. They were also to report the number of marriages celebrated each year after 1754. On the basis of these figures Rickman made his own estimates of the total size of England's population and of its counties at various dates in the eighteenth century. Many others followed—Malthus, Finlaison, Farr, Brownlee, Talbot Griffith, more recently Deane and Cole. Although their techniques may differ, all rely on the data contained in Rickman's Parish Abstracts. Sadly, the original manuscripts of Rickman's inquiry no longer survive. We have no way of knowing whether all parishes in England and Wales returned the required information, what procedures Rickman followed to overcome deficiencies (if any), or how efficiently individual parish clergyman counted the entries in their registers. Moreover, it is not comforting to find that many of the years for which Rickman's data are available before 1780 are quite atypical of 'normal' demographic experience. The turn of each decade was all too often marked by abnormally low numbers of baptisms and marriages and by unusually high numbers of burials—a characteristic which might upset even the most carefully designed estimates of population size based upon them.

Rickman's published returns, moreover, relate only to national or county units. For small areas, analyses of variations in the size and rate of growth of population depend entirely on the first-hand study of surviving parish registers. While such studies avoid the obvious weaknesses of the Parish Register Abstracts, they share with Rickman's figures the oft-repeated failings of the parish registers as sources for demographic history. These failings will be discussed more fully in the following section on natural increase and migration. It is enough to note here that in certain parts of the country, and especially during the late eighteenth and early nineteenth centuries, the parish register returns of baptisms, marriages and burials significantly understate the true number of births, marriages and deaths in the population. The strain which this places on our estimates of population size and population growth rates can be easily imagined. Sadly, not all of the studies so far available to us have bothered properly to quantify its significance.

Serious though all these shortcomings are, they do not totally negate the value of the available estimates of national and county population size based on the Parish Register Abstracts, nor those of regional or local population size derived from the first-hand study of extant parish registers. Clearly, however, all such estimates should be approached with caution. This is especially the case with the national and county population totals derived from the Parish Register Abstracts. Regional or local population estimates are usually more accurate provided they have been compiled with the necessary care. In theory (if not always the case in practice), local analyses are in a position to work on only those registers which seem to be relatively free of the worst deficiencies to which the parish registers were subject, and may be able to minimise serious difficulties should any occur.

Apart from the parish registers, the only other source for estimating the size and growth rate of the population before the introduction of the civil census in 1801 is the information contained in surviving 'listings of inhabitants'. The content and breadth of coverage of individual listings varies enormously as the several examples included with this chapter demonstrate. Two characteristics are common to most of them, however. First, no extant 'listing' covers the whole of England and Wales. A few do indeed incorporate quite large population groups. But most of the more detailed and more reliable 'listings' relate only to very small areas and populations. Second, the overwhelming majority of seventeenth- and eighteenth-century 'listings' were not intended for demographic purposes by their compilers. The ones which have until recently been most frequently used by historical demographers (the Hearth Tax returns of the late seventeenth century, the Compton census of 1676, and the Ecclesiastical Visitations of the eighteenth century) were designed for purely fiscal or religious purposes. A brief look at each of these three sources will illustrate some of the problems in using them as materials for population history.

The Hearth Tax, begun in 1662 and abolished in 1688, was collected from all households with an income above a certain minimum level, and varied in amount according to the number of firehearths and stoves each household contained. Theoretically, Hearth Tax returns should record the name of the occupying head of each household whether he paid tax or not. It is this list of household heads which provides the raw material for historical demographers. If it were complete, a single multiplication of the total number of household heads by a figure representing the average number of persons in each household would give a reasonable guide to the size of the total population. Unfortunately, the reality is less straightforward. Many of the surviving returns were badly entered or illegibly written. Others have been poorly preserved. In others the list of persons exempt from payment is missing. Tax lists of this type cannot be used for

Aspley guise   May the 5th   1694

An Assessment made by the Assessors of Aspley guise in the County of Beds. for moneys payable to theire Maiesties by virtue of an act of parliament made and instituted an act for raiseing mony by a poll payable quarterly for one yeare for Carrying on a vigorous war against ffrance.

	£	s
William Norcliffe esq. and his Wife	1	2
Henry Maninge Servant to Mr Norcliffe	0	1
Sarah Lambe Servant to Mr Norcliffe	0	1
Mary Haddock Servant to Mr Norcliffe	0	1
Edward Hall and Mary his Wife	1	2
Joseph Hall Son of Edward	0	1
Thomas Hall Son of Mr Hall	0	1
Hannah Willomot Servant of Mr Hall	0	1
Edward Worster and his Wife	0	2
Edward Worster Son of Edward	0	1
Thomas Worster Son of Edward	0	1
Elizabeth Ffidgings Servant to Edward Worster	0	1

	£	s
John Gurney and his grandmother	0	2
Richard Wall Servant to John Gurney	0	1
Ann Willomot Servant to Jo: Gurney	0	1
Elizabeth Gillott Widd	0	1

Extract from Aspley Guise, Bedfordshire, 'Listing of Inhabitants', 1694.

demographic purposes. But there are difficulties even with those Hearth Tax returns which appear to have been carefully compiled and which have stood the test of time relatively well. Taxation is never popular and in the seventeenth century when tax collection was less efficient than it is today there must have been a good deal of successful evasion. As a result, all studies of population size based on taxation returns undoubtedly understate its true level. But by how much? Since there is no way of estimating the number of people who evaded registration and payment (and who would, therefore, not appear in the tax lists) we cannot tell. All that can be said with any safety is that population estimates derived from taxation returns understate the truth to an unknown, immeasurable extent. Even then there remains one final problem associated with the use of Hearth Tax lists—that of converting the number of household heads given by each list into an estimate of total population size. To do this we require a multiplier which accurately represents the average number of occupants in each houshold. Because the size of the household varied considerably from one area and one social group to another the accuracy of the multiplier is clearly crucial. Unfortunately, until very recently, evidence on regional variations in average household size has been scarce. Most of the available estimates of aggregate population based on Heath Tax returns have relied for their multiplier on the figures supplied by Gregory King for the late seventeenth century. For work on the population of rural areas, for example, historical demographers have normally used King's estimate of $4\frac{1}{2}$ persons per household. However accurate this may or may not prove to be the fact is that it is an average which obscures wide regional divergencies even in rural areas. Mean household size differed greatly even between areas of similar economic structure and between population groups of similar size. The average number of persons per household in twenty-one small Westmorland villages and hamlets during the late eighteenth century ranged from a low of 3.63 to a high of 6.50, though the mean (4.7) comes out quite close to King's approximation (P. Laslett, 'The size and structure of the household in England over three centuries', *Population Studies*, XXIII, 2, 1969). In eight small Kent parishes in 1705 it ranged from 4.00 to 5.58, with a mean of 4.6. It may prove that studies of the population of fairly large rural areas are quite justified in relying on Gregory King's figure of

$4\frac{1}{2}$ persons per household. But those which relate only to small groups of parishes or, what is worse, to the single parish are much less likely to be reliable if they assume a mean household size of $4\frac{1}{2}$ persons without adequate justification.

Both the Compton census of 1676 and the visitations of the eighteenth century were ecclesiastical surveys, though of rather different types. The Compton census, which was apparently taken only in the province of Canterbury, set out to record the total number of Anglican Conformists, Protestant Non-conformists and Papists aged sixteen years and above in each parish. The visitations were replies made by local parish incumbents to lists of queries sent out by the diocesan authorities preparatory to a visitation of the parish. Among the questions included was one asking for information on the number of 'families' living in the parish. By calculating the proportion of the population likely to be below sixteen years of age (in the case of the Compton census), or by devising a multiplier representative of the average number of persons in each 'family' (in the case of the visitations) both sources can be made to yield information on the total size of the population. Once again, however, there are certain practical difficulties which should not be overlooked. Reliable data on regional and chronological variations in 'family' size and age-structures are only now becoming available in any abundance. Most of the studies upon whose findings we rely have been compiled without the benefit of such sophisticated information. Some of their 'guesstimates' may turn out to be wildly inaccurate. Moreover, in the final analysis, the reliability of religious censuses depends on the zeal and efficiency of the individual parish clergyman. No doubt many were highly conscientious but many others certainly were not. In large parishes particularly, their returns may often have been little more than guesswork. The usual assumption that the Compton census is a better guide to the size of the population than the contemporary Hearth Tax may well be correct, but the subsequent ecclesiastical listings of the eighteenth century become much less useful in the face of growing clerical laxity and rapidly increasing population.

Like those based on parish register data, estimates of population size derived from Hearth Tax or religious censuses of the type described above are useful only if they have been compiled with obvious care, and even then only after due allowance has been made for the fact that they can never be more than approximations to the truth.

In recent years historians have unearthed many other kinds of 'listings' which contain information on the size of local populations. Some, like those carried out in preparation for the William and Mary tax of 1695–1705, had fiscal purposes. Others, like the Rector's book of the parish of Clayworth in Nottinghamshire, had ecclesiastical origins. But it is becoming clear that countless other local population censuses have survived, particularly for the later part of the eighteenth century—those designed as part of public health inquiries, as aids to local government, town map-making and estate-surveying, even some which were specifically motivated by a growing interest in the population question itself (see the thorough discussion in C. M. Law, *Population Studies*, XXIII, 1, 1969). When these sources have been fully tapped, our knowledge of regional variations in the rate of population growth will become much more comprehensive than it is at the moment. In the meantime, however, regional estimates of population size based on listings of inhabitants must continue to depend on the less detailed and less reliable Hearth Tax, Compton census and Visitation returns. Indeed, for large population groups and broad geographic areas they may always have to do so since most of

---

An Accurate Review of all the Families in Renholdt Parish or otherwise Dependent on The Estate of John Becher Esq., including Farmers Tenants Cottagers Labourers Dependents etc., containing a comprehensive Account of their several Characters which were searched into with indefatigable Industry & with vast Judgements & Penetration & are now set forth with uncommon Precision this Month of June A.D. 1773.

		(Character) The better for the above Estate
John Becher his Wife & Son with 10 Men & Maid Servants . . . . Sum total	13	
Tho. Dickinson, Wife & 8 Serv[ts]	10	Industrious & Rich
Tho. Street his Wife 7 Children 2 Serv[ts]	11	An industrious thriving good Family
Rob[t] Newman 4 Children 3 Serv[ts]	8	An industrious good family
Chas. Ellis 2 Sons Wife 4 Serv[ts]	8	Industrious & thriving – Goldington
Henry Sassinger His Wife 2 Children 6 Serv[ts]	10	Ditto Such an odd Dog
Henry Bull Wife 6 Children 2 Serv[ts]	10	Ditto
Robert Wootton 4 Children 2 Serv[ts]	7	Old Honest good family
Joseph Hull Housekeeper 3 Serv[ts]	5	Good farmer & an honest fellow, very kind to his housekeeper
John Smith Jun. Wife 2 Children 4 Serv[ts]	8	A notorious fidler, & an idle thoughtless young man
— Street Jun. Wife 1 Child 2 Serv[ts]	5	Good young People likely to do well later
John Smith Sen. his Wife 3 Children 1 Serv[t]	6	Good farmer & industrious Wife but ill match'd not withstanding
Henry Woodward housekeeper & keeps a Cow	2	Industrious & thriving
Thomas Field 2 Sisters 2 Brothers & a Cow	5	(without the cow) Young (Bricklayer) & with assistar likely to retrieve their father's losses
Benj. Jeffreys Wife Son 4 Serv[ts]	7	Industrious & good
Rob. Goddard his Wife 6 Children & a Cow	8	Blacksmith will do well if he can with so large a family

Extract from Renhold, Bedfordshire, 'Listing of Inhabitants', 1773.

the detailed 'listings' refer to small population units only, often no bigger than the individual parish. Perhaps the greatest contribution which the detailed 'listings of inhabitants' will make to the future development of historical demography will be the provision of accurate data on variations in household and 'family' size and in the proportion of the population falling below the age of sixteen years—data which can be used to rework the material contained in geographically more extensive but qualitatively less adequate taxation and ecclesiastical documents.

Any source-material which is used to construct estimates of national or regional population size should ideally provide a complete coverage of the population group concerned. If it does not do so, we must at the very least be able to devise satisfactory techniques for including those sections of the community which have been omitted. Few seventeenth- and eighteenth-century sources and methods of analysis strictly meet these two requirements. Accordingly, all population estimates based upon them should be approached with caution.

2. *Natural Increase and Migration*

The size and rate of growth of any population is a function of alterations in the rate of natural increase and in the balance between in- and out-migration.

Before the introduction of civil registration in 1837 our knowledge of regional and chronological variations in the pace of natural increase depends on the returns of baptisms and burials given in the parish registers of the Established Church. At first sight these provide us with much of the information we might need. Before 1780, as we have seen, national and county estimates of the number of baptisms and burials are available in Rickman's Parish Register Abstracts for selected years only (1700–01, 1710–11, 1720–21 etc.), but thereafter they are available annually. In theory, therefore, we should be able to trace the yearly evolution of national and county natural increase rates throughout the entire period from 1780 to 1837. For the period before 1780 and for areas smaller than the county unit or crossing county boundaries the pattern of natural increase might instead be derived from a first-hand analysis of some of the large number of parish registers which still survive. In reality, however, the exercise is not so simple. The reliability of the parish registers themselves has long been in doubt. Do they fully cover the populations they claim to? Was every birth and death which occurred in the parish always faithfully entered in the Anglican baptism and burial registers? Sadly, the answer to both these questions must be no. Although most marriages found their way into the registers, many births and deaths quite clearly did not.

The problem of underregistration in the parish registers of the eighteenth and early nineteenth centuries is related to three developments: the rise of secularism and a growing disinterest in religious observance, exemplified on the one hand by declining clerical zeal and an increase in pluralism and absenteeism, and on the other by lessening popular interest in the services and sacraments of the Established Church; the rapid geographic redistribution of the population (the result of regional variations in the pace of economic development) which led to the growth of large urban populations in areas that were inadequately served by the Anglican church; and finally, the spread of the Protestant Nonconformist religion. If the extent of underregistration had remained consistent over time and between one area and another the problem would not be too serious. While we could not rely on the baptism and burial entries to give us the precise level of natural increase rates, they might still be useful guides to the general trends in such rates. Sadly, the degree of underregistration was not consistent; it varied greatly from area to area, and was particularly serious in the newly-emergent urban-manufacturing centres of the early Industrial Revolution and in communities with a high proportion of religious dissenters. Moreover, its incidence varied in a complex fashion between the baptism and the burial registers. Before about 1800, because there were few Nonconformist burial grounds outside the London area, underregistration was more common in baptism than burial registers. As a result, at least outside London and its environs, the rate of natural increase is usually understated by the parish register aggregates of baptisms and burials. A similar pattern of underregistration prevailed in the first decade of the nineteenth century, and again after 1820. For these periods also we can assume that natural increase rates were somewhat higher than the parish register entries suggest. In the decade 1810–20 however, for reasons fully and convincingly discussed by Professor Krause, the 'normal' pattern of underregistration was temporarily reversed.

1st Jany. 1782   1.
CARDINGTON
Cottage No. 1.

		Age Y. M. D.
Occupier	Essex Hartop, Labr. Born at Keysor ⎫	43 – –
Wife	Elizabeth, Maiden-name Billen, Born ⎬	
	at Cardington And late Wid<u>w</u> of ⎭	
	William Urine. S.L.	46 – –
Children	By first Husband viz.	
1st	Elizabeth, Married at Warden	27 – –
2nd	Hannah, Married at Meppershall	24 – –
Children	By her Present Husband, viz.	
3rd	Thomas, Works for Mr Whibread	17 – –
4th	Mary	16 – –
		Y. M. D.
5th	Phebe S.L.	14 – –
6th	Joseph-billen at School by Mr Howard	10 – –

Note, That S.L. means Spins Linen, S.J. Spins
Jersey, S.L. and J. Spins Linen & Jersey; and
M.L. makes Lace.

Extract from Cardington 'Listing of Inhabitants', 1782.

Briefly, the number of deaths omitted from the registers exceeded
that of births. In the 1810s, therefore, parish register totals of
baptisms and burials may well exaggerate the true level of natural
increase rates. All of the above, based on the work of Professor
Krause (in Glass and Eversley (eds.), *Population in History*) is
highly conjectural. But it is enough to persuade us to approach
the problem of underregistration and its effects on variations in
the rate of natural increase with considerable care.

The problem of omission from the church registers has long
been recognized and numerous attempts have been made to
correct for it. Most popular has been the use of 'omission-ratios'
derived for the late 1830s from a comparison of the number of

baptisms, burials and marriages in the parish registers with the number of births, deaths and marriages given in the civil returns of the Registrar-General. These ratios are then used to correct the deficient baptism and burial totals of earlier years. Unfortunately, this exercise raises more problems than it solves. As we have seen the extent of omission from the registers varied considerably from time to time and from one area to another. Underregistration, and therefore the ratios required to correct for it, was greater in the late 1830s than for any period up to about 1790 but much smaller than it had been between 1790 and 1820. To apply a 'correction-ratio' devised for the 1830s to the parish register data of earlier periods is obviously unwise.

In view of the difficulty involved in correcting for the underregistration of baptisms and burials in the eighteenth and early nineteenth centuries, some demographic historians have felt it best to ignore the problem altogether. For those parts of the country where the size of the population changed very little and where the number of religious dissenters remained small—where, in other words, the problem of underregistration never became significant—this is quite acceptable. But it is clearly unjustified elsewhere. Since the areas of most rapid population growth and extensive Nonconformist congregations are the ones of greatest interest to historians of early industrial England it is imperative that better methods of dealing with the problem of underregistration in such areas are devised. In the meantime we must judge existing analyses of regional and periodic variations in rates of natural increase before 1837 with a cautious eye on the possible effects of underregistration on their conclusions.

Until passenger lists, census and civil registration returns become available in the mid-nineteenth century there is no way of measuring the extent of variations in the balance of migration into and out of England and Wales as a whole. Fortunately, in regard to the movement of people *within* the country during the eighteenth and early nineteenth centuries we are rather better served by our source-materials. Some indication, if only a crude one, of the frequency and direction of internal migration can be gleaned from data contained in parish registers and in nominal lists of various kinds.

The parish registers can be used to measure the extent of popular geographic mobility in two ways: the first involves a calculation of the degree to which a given set of surnames survives in the register entries over a period of years; the second requires a simple analysis of the statements regarding place of last residence given by brides and grooms in the more detailed marriage registers. Both procedures are far from infallible. The inadequacies of the first are particularly obvious. Given the limited range of surnames then in common use, the survival of a particular name over a number of years cannot always be taken to imply the continued residence of the same individual or family. It is conceivable, for instance, that the original John Smith had died or moved elsewhere and had been replaced in later register entries by a newcomer of the same name. Nor is there any reason to assume that the disappearance of a particular name from a register was always due to the emigration of the person concerned. It could as easily be due to his death. Analyses of migratory habits based on statements of previous residence in the marriage registers are more rewarding, provided that the entries are made consistently and unambiguously. Even so, they should be treated with care. Professor Chambers long ago drew our attention to parishes which for one reason or another had become popular marriage centres. Many of the couples marrying in such parishes had never lived there and had no intention of living there in the future. Quite a false impression of the frequency and pattern of internal migration would emerge from an analysis based on the marriage registers of parishes like these.

The migration of people within England and Wales during the eighteenth and early nineteenth centuries can also be studied from data contained in nominal lists of one kind or another—taxation returns, the rolls of gilds and corporations, and the more detailed census-type 'listings of inhabitants'. Where successive tax lists or nominal rolls still survive, a comparison of recorded surnames will give a rough indication of the rate of popular movement over a period of time. Like the similar procedure based on parish register data, this suffers from the limited range of surnames then in use, and from the fact that the disappearance of a name in a later list may mean the death rather than the emigration of the individual concerned. Additionally surnames may disappear from subsequent taxation lists simply because a person had fallen below the minimum income level at which tax was paid or because he had successfully managed to avoid payment. Finally, it is worth remembering that people represented in taxation returns and even more so those named in the rolls of gilds and corporations, come from a very narrow range of social classes. Their migratory habits may be very different from those of the population at large. Perhaps after all the best hope for reliable information on internal migration will stem from future analyses of the detailed, census-type 'listings of inhabitants' like that for the Bedfordshire parish of Cardington, a section of which is reproduced with this chapter. Documents of this type, giving place of birth and present whereabouts, may one day help us to quantify with some precision the extent and direction of popular movement during the eighteenth and early nineteenth centuries.

3. Nuptiality, Fertility and Mortality

We began this chapter by emphasising that a complete under-standing of the complex, two-way relationship between popula-tion growth and economic and social development requires information not only on the size and rate of growth of a popula-tion, and on variations in the rate of natural increase and migra-tion, but also on trends in the levels of fertility and mortality as well as in what we might call the socio-demographic structure of the population (i.e. age, sex, marital, household and family structure). The possible sources of information on the socio-demographic composition of a population in the period before census enumerators' books become available will be discussed in Chapter VI. Let us for the moment concentrate on the ways and means of providing information on nuptiality, fertility and mortality rates during the eighteenth and early nineteenth centuries.

Until the advent of civil registration in 1837, for data on variations in the vital rates we are forced once again to rely on the parish register returns of baptism, burials and marriages. Most of the available studies have used what Dr Eversley has called 'the aggregative technique of analysis'—a technique which guarantees a fairly rapid and substantial return of information relative to the effort required. Among other things, aggregative analysis yields data on crude birth- and marriage-rates, and on crude death-rates by sex (i.e. the number of births, marriages and deaths per thousand total population—assuming, of course, that we know what the size of the population was): on the average number of

baptisms (births) per marriage (by means of a simple division of
the total number of marriages into the total number of baptisms
for any one period); on the frequency of female celibacy (based
on the number of women described as unmarried in the burial
registers expressed as a proportion of total adult female deaths);
on age at marriage (from statements of age which are occasionally
found in some of the better marriage registers); on the extent of
illegitimacy (from entries in both baptism and burial registers);
and finally on rates of mortality by age-group (based on those
burial registers which clearly distinguish between infants, children
and adults, or much more rarely on those which record a specific
age at death).

The material which can be extracted from the parish registers
using unsophisticated aggregative techniques is certainly useful.
But it is not as informative nor as reliable as demographic historians require. Crude birth-, death- and marriage-rates are only
rough and ready guides to changing patterns of fertility, mortality
and nuptiality because they make no allowance for regional and
periodic differences in age, sex and marital structures. Neither can
the true level of marital fertility be accurately measured by a
simple division of the number of baptisms by the number of
marriages. As a general rule, because the problem of underregistration was more serious in baptism than marriage registers,
our derived baptisms per marriage quotients will be far too low,
unless of course careful allowance has been made for under-
enumeration. Moreover, the emigration of people from parishes
in which their marriages were celebrated to parishes in which
their children were baptised may further distort the real pattern of
local variations in the average number of baptisms per marriage.
The accuracy of specific statements of illegitimacy and female
celibacy obviously depends on having register entries which consistently record such details, and this was all too rare. Ages at
marriage and death were not often given in English parish registers
and, as family reconstitution studies have shown, those that are
recorded are not always absolutely accurate. Although burial
registers usually give a rough indication for any one period of the
proportion of total deaths which occurred during infancy, child-
hood or adulthood, they do not permit a thorough analysis of the
mortality experience of each age-group over time. The point of all
this is simply to demonstrate that though the well-tried techniques

of aggregative analysis yield a certain amount of valuable material they do not provide enough reliable population data to meet the refined needs of a detailed demographic exercise. For data of such sophistication we must turn to the recently developed techniques of family reconstitution.

The application of family reconstitution procedures to parish register material was first attempted on a grand scale in France by Professor Louis Henry. His methods have been modified to meet the particular requirements of English parish registers by Dr Wrigley and the Cambridge Group for the History of Population and Social Structure.

In theory, the range of demographic data which can be extracted from the parish register entries of baptisms, burials and marriages via the reconstruction of family groups is extremely impressive: the age at, and duration of, marriage; the frequency of adult celibacy, both among males and females; the average interval between the date of marriage and the birth of the first child, and between successive births; the average duration of the child-bearing period; the number of multiple births; the proportion of children born illegitimate; the average number of births per marriage or by age-group of a woman within marriage; the sex-ratio of births; mortality rates by age-group and sex; life expectancy at various ages. Where this type of information can be combined with that derived from 'listings of inhabitants' (on age and sex structure, marital status, migratory habits, household and family size and composition) an analysis of the relationship between population, economy and society would be very thorough indeed.

So far the only major published study based on family reconstitution techniques has been that for the Devonshire parish of Colyton (E. A. Wrigley, *Economic History Review*, XIX, 1966, and *Daedalus*, 97, 1968). But others are under way, and the future appears to hold exciting prospects. In view of the attention lavished on family reconstitution as the key which will unravel the mysteries of pre-industrial population change, it is particularly important for us to satisfy ourselves that the new technique is fully capable of supporting the hopes placed upon it.

The accuracy of family reconstitution data depends on the adequacy of the parish registers that are used. Each entry in the register must be sufficiently detailed to allow the reliable identi-

fication of individuals despite the limited range of personal names
then in use. We must, for example, be able to say with a reasonable degree of certainty that the John Brown baptised in 1700
was the same person as the John Brown who was married in 1725
and who died in 1760. Otherwise it will prove impossible to
allocate individuals to their proper family groups. On the whole,
although English parish registers are considerably less detailed
than their French equivalents, they are normally adequate for
reconstitution purposes. Baptism entries usually give the christian
names of the baptised, the date of baptism (though rarely of
birth), and the christian name and surname of the father or father
and mother, e.g. John son of Dan (and Mary) Brown. The
marriage registers record the date of marriage and the full names
of both bride and groom, and often additional information on
place of last permanent residence, marital status (whether single,
or widowed), and age (though usually only in cases where the
bride or groom was below twenty-one years of age, when the
description 'minor' might be appended). The burial registers
give date of burial. If the burial is that of a child, the names of
its father or father and mother are usually given, e.g. John son of
Dan (and Mary) Brown; if that of a woman her marital status is
normally recorded, e.g. Mary wife of Dan Brown, Mary Brown
widow (where the name only of a deceased woman is given, e.g.
Mary Brown, it is usually safe to assume that she died unmarried—
sometimes indeed the description 'singlewoman' is attached). For
adult males, however, burial entries can often be less precise,
frequently giving only the date of burial and full name of the
deceased, e.g. Dan Brown. This may occasionally result in a
confusion of identities—where, for example, grandfather, father
and son all of the christian name Dan are alive at the same time.
But in smaller parishes with reasonably detailed registers this
dilemma can usually be resolved.

For most small, rural parishes—in other words for most of the
parishes in England and Wales—the application of family reconstitution procedures to registers of this kind will ultimately
provide much accurate and highly detailed demographic information. It must, however, be emphasised that many English parish
registers were not as thoroughly documented as this, and that the
entry-quality of some of even the better registers frequently
deteriorated in the course of time.

The parish registers of large urban populations, where the problems of personal identification are in any case compounded by the constant inward stream of migrants, are of a notoriously poor quality. So too are some of those in communities with large numbers of religious Dissenters. Even in many small rural parishes, where the quality and quantity of register entries had previously been adequate for reconstitution purposes, there was a significant decline in standards during the late eighteenth and early nineteenth centuries. Burial entries particularly often degenerated into nothing more than a list of names, e.g. John Brown, Mary Brown, Dan Brown. The reliable identification of individuals necessary for a careful family reconstitution analysis is extremely difficult in such cases. Sadly it is in the areas and periods of greatest interest to the historian of economic, social and demographic change that the registers are likely to prove less suitable for the application of family reconstitution techniques. Only time will tell whether they can be satisfactorily applied to the registers of large and rapidly-growing urban-manufacturing populations, particularly those of the late eighteenth and early nineteenth centuries. At the moment one is forced to admit that the difficulties look unsurmountable.

* * *

How adequate then are the population statistics upon which we must rely? From about the middle of the nineteenth century—more specifically from the inauguration of civil registration in 1837 and the improvement in methods of census-taking in 1841—they are extensive and reliable enough to meet most of the needs of historical demographic analysis. Unfortunately, this is not true of the statistics which are available for the eighteenth and early nineteenth centuries. These latter are much less complete and far less reliable. Conceivably, the application of new techniques in the future, like that of family reconstitution, will fill some of the existing gaps and provide rather better data with which to work. But for the time being anyway, any analysis of the relationship between population, economic and social change during the period of England's early industrialisation is doomed to be relatively tentative, unsophisticated and incomplete, and should be treated as such.

FURTHER READING

Books and Monographs

B. Benjamin, *Demographic Analysis*, London, 1968.

L. Bradley, 'A glossary for local population studies', *Local Population Studies Supplement*, January, 1971.

N. H. Carrier and J. R. Jeffrey, 'External migration—a study of the available statistics, 1815–1950', *General Register Office Studies in Medical and Population Subjects*, No. 6, HMSO, London, 1953.

P. R. Cox, *Demography*, 3rd ed., Cambridge University Press, 1959.

I. Ferenczi and W. F. Willcox, *International Migration*, New York, 1929–31, 2 vols.

B. R. Mitchell and P. Deane, *Abstract of British Historical Statistics*, Cambridge University Press, 1962.

L. Munby, *Hertfordshire Population Statistics, 1563–1801*, Hitchin, 1964.

M. P. Newton and J. R. Jeffrey, 'Internal migration—some aspects of population movements within England and Wales', *General Register Office Studies in Medical and Population Subjects*, No. 5, HMSO, London, 1951.

B. Thomas, *Migration and Economic Growth*, Cambridge University Press, 1954.

E. A. Wrigley (ed.), *An Introduction to English Historical Demography*, London, 1966.

E. A. Wrigley (ed.), *Nineteenth Century Society*, Cambridge University Press, 1972.

Articles

E. J. Buckatzsch, 'The constancy of local populations and migration in England before 1800', *Population Studies*, V, I, 1951–52.

D. V. Glass, 'A note on the under-registration of births in Britain in the nineteenth century', *Population Studies*, V, I, 1951–52.

D. V. Glass, 'Population movements in England and Wales 1700–1850', in D. V. Glass and D. E. C. Eversley (eds.), *Population in History*, London, 1965.

D. V. Glass, 'Two papers on Gregory King', ibid.

L. Henry, 'The verification of data in historical demography', *Population Studies*, XXII, I, 1968.

J. T. Krause, 'The changing adequacy of English registration 1690–1837', in Glass and Eversley, op. cit.

C. M. Law, 'Local censuses in the 18th century', *Population Studies*, XXIII, I, 1969.

J. Taylor, 'The taking of the census 1801–1951', *British Medical Journal*, April 1951.

J. Thirsk, 'Sources of information on population, 1500–1760', II, *The Amateur Historian*, 4 May 1959.

2. The Growth of Population, 1695-1939

What has been the general pattern of English population growth since the late seventeenth century? How closely has the demographic experience of England and Wales reflected that of Western Europe as a whole? To what extent have recent English population trends been determined by variations in the levels of fertility, mortality or migration? These are the questions with which we will be concerned in this chapter.

1. Population Growth and Distribution

Some of the more reliable estimates of the size and rate of growth of England's population since 1695 are given in Table I below. Those from 1801 onwards are based on decennial civil census returns and can be regarded as accurate. Those for the eighteenth century, based on data contained in the Parish Register Abstracts of baptisms, burials and marriages, are rather less satisfactory, but probably reliable enough for the present purpose.

TABLE I *The Population of England and Wales, 1695-1939*

Date	Population (millions)	Rate of Growth (%per annum)	
1695	5.2		
1701	5.8	1695–1701	1.2
1711	6.0	1701–1711	0.3
1721	6.0	1711–1721	0.1
1731	6.1	1721–1731	0.1
1741	6.2	1731–1741	0.2
1751	6.5	1741–1751	0.4
1761	6.7	1751–1761	0.4
1771	7.2	1761–1771	0.6
1781	7.5	1771–1781	0.5
1791	8.3	1781–1791	1.0
1801	9.2	1791–1801	1.1
1811	10.2	1801–1811	1.1

Date	Population (millions)	Rate of Growth (% per annum)	
1821	12.0	1811–1821	1.8
1831	13.9	1821–1831	1.6
1841	15.9	1831–1841	1.4
1851	17.9	1841–1851	1.3
1861	20.1	1851–1861	1.2
1871	22.7	1861–1871	1.3
1881	26.0	1871–1881	1.4
1891	29.0	1881–1891	1.2
1901	32.5	1891–1901	1.2
1911	36.1	1901–1911	1.1
1921	37.9	1911–1921	0.5
1931	40.0	1921–1931	0.6
1939	41.5	1931–1939	0.4

Sources:

1695—D. V. Glass, 'Gregory King's estimate of the population of England and Wales, 1695', *Population Studies*, II, 1950.

1701, 1781 and 1801—P. Deane and W. A. Cole, *British Economic Growth*, 1688–1959, 2nd ed., Cambridge University Press, 1967.

1711–1771 inclusive—G. S. L. Tucker, 'English pre-industrial population trends', *Economic History Review*, 2nd ser., XVI, 2, 1963.

1791—'J. Brownlee, History of the birth and death-rates in England and Wales . . .' *Public Health*, June and July, 1916.

1811–1939 inclusive—B. R. Mitchell and P. Deane, *Abstract of British Historical Statistics*, Cambridge University Press, 1962.

In the two-and-a-half centuries between Gregory King's estimate for 1695 and the Registrar-General's mid-year estimate for 1939, the population of England and Wales rose eightfold, from 5.2 to 41.5 million.

There were, as Table I shows, considerable short-term fluctuations in the average annual rate of population increase within this long period. Throughout the first half of the eighteenth century, especially during the three decades between 1711 and 1740, population grew very slowly. Then in the period from the 1740s to the 1770s the pace of demographic increase accelerated. By comparison with what was to follow, however, it remained fairly modest. Beginning in the decade 1781–90, as Professor Tucker

(*Economic History Review*, XVI, 1963) has already convincingly demonstrated, the rate of English population growth accelerated dramatically. It was twice as high in the 1780s and 1790s than it had been in the 1770s. Thereafter, throughout most of the first half of the nineteenth century, the rate of population increase averaged 1.5% per annum, three times greater than that achieved between 1740 and 1780. Although it fell slightly after 1850, population continued to grow at a rate of between 1% and 1.5% a year right down to the outbreak of the First World War. This is the period, from the late eighteenth to the early twentieth century, which historians have christened 'population revolution'. Never before had such high rates of demographic increase been maintained for so long. Almost as suddenly as it had begun, however, the era of rapid population growth came to an end in the second decade of the twentieth century. In the thirty-year period bounded by the two world wars the pace of population growth fell abruptly to about 0.5% per annum—a level very similar to that in the three decades before 1780, though still well above that of the first half of the eighteenth century.

Although there have, of course, been marked variations in rates of population growth from one country to another (see Table II), the overall pattern of English population increase since the late seventeenth century has borne a remarkable resemblance to that observed elsewhere in Western Europe.

TABLE II *The Rate of Population Growth in Western European Countries Annual Average Percentage Increase*

Country	1700–1750	1750–1800	1800–1850	1850–1910	1910–1940
England/Wales	0.2	0.7	1.8	1.6	0.5
France	0.1	0.6	0.7	0.2	0.1
Holland	0.7	0.8	0.8	1.5	1.7
Belgium	0.8	0.7	0.9	1.2	0.4
Sweden	–	0.6	1.0	1.0	0.5
Scotland	0.6	0.5	1.6	0.9	0.4
Ireland	0.6	1.1	0.6	0.6	0.1
Denmark	–	0.3	1.6	1.4	1.0
Finland	–	3.0	1.2	1.6	0.6
Norway	0.4	1.0	1.3	1.0	0.8

Population statistics for European countries in the early eighteenth century are unfortunately rare and not altogether reliable. But those which do exist confirm that the first half of the century was an era of general demographic stagnation. The population of France rose from only 20 to 21 million between 1700 and 1750: that of Norway grew at the slender rate of 0.4% per annum before the 1750s: in Denmark the rate of population increase stayed as low as 0.2% per annum until the mid-1770s: although Swedish population increased rapidly by 1.1% per annum between 1721 and 1735, it had not grown at all in the first twenty years of the century, and in the period 1735–50 averaged a mere 0.2% a year: in Scotland, Belgium, Holland and Ireland rates of demographic increase were somewhat higher, but even here they fell short of the levels which were to be reached in the second half of the eighteenth or early nineteenth centuries (Holland and Belgium only marginally so).

At some stage after the middle of the eighteenth century the pace of population increase quickened in all Western European societies, though the beginnings of population 'take-off' did vary

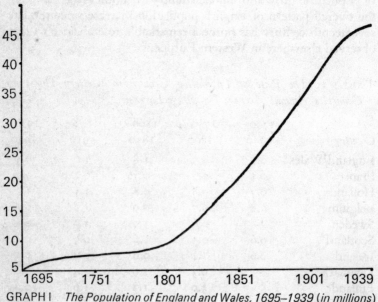

GRAPH I   *The Population of England and Wales, 1695–1939 (in millions)*

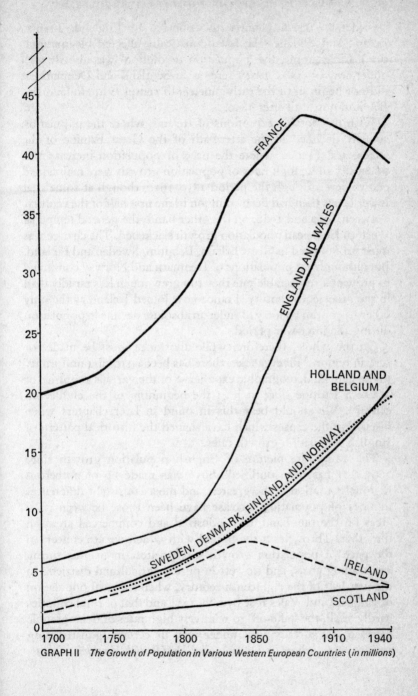

GRAPH II   *The Growth of Population in Various Western European Countries* (*in millions*)

considerably from country to country. In England, France, Ireland and Finland (the last dramatically affected by immigration), for example, the 'population revolution' was already well under way by 1800. Elsewhere, as in Scotland and Denmark, it did not begin until the early nineteenth century: in Holland and Belgium not until after 1850.

With the notable exceptions of Ireland, where the population actually declined in the aftermath of the Great Famine of the 1840s, and France, where the pace of population increase was unusually slow, high rates of population growth were maintained everywhere through the period 1850–1910, though at somewhat lower levels than had been common in the first half of the century. Between 1910 and 1940, on the other hand, the general tempo of Western European population growth slackened. The change was most pronounced in Great Britain, Belgium, Sweden and Finland. But although the populations of Denmark and Norway continued to grow at a respectable rate they too grew much less rapidly than in the nineteenth century. France now joined Ireland as the only other European country to suffer an absolute decline in population during the inter-war period.

On the whole, therefore, while allowance must be made for certain regional divergencies, there has been a striking uniformity in the general demographic experience of the various countries of Western Europe since at least the beginning of the eighteenth century. We should bear this in mind in later chapters when discussing the causes which have shaped the historical pattern of English population growth rates.

The composite picture of English population growth since 1695 that has been outlined above was made up of numerous regional variations. The greatest and most consistent differences in rates of population increase have been those between rural areas on the one hand, and industrial and commercial areas on the other. Throughout the period with which we are concerned the pace of population growth was greatest in manufacturing and trading areas, and slowest in purely agricultural districts. In the first half of the eighteenth century, when the total population of England and Wales rose by only 12% and that of rural counties hardly at all, the 'take-off' to relatively high rates of demographic increase was already well under way in certain industrialising regions. According to Deane and Cole (*British Economic Growth*,

1688–1959) the populations of Lancashire, Warwickshire and the West Riding of Yorkshire increased by 33%, 28% and 26% respectively between 1701 and 1751. Even that of an old industrial county like Gloucestershire, in the heart of the West Country textile area, grew by over 30% at a time when the population of England and Wales as a whole was generally static. Confirmation of abnormally high rates of population increase in manufacturing areas during the early eighteenth century is provided by the various regional analyses now available to us. In twelve parishes around Bromsgrove (Worcestershire)—parishes which became at least partly industrialised in the course of the eighteenth and early nineteenth centuries—the estimated population rose from 7,167 in 1700 to 9,018 in 1750, an increase of 25%–26% (Eversley, *Population Studies*, X, 1957). In seventeen parishes centring on the Shropshire village of Coalbrookdale where Abraham Darby founded his famous iron works in 1709, the population leapt from 11,500 in 1711 to 17,326 in 1750, an average annual growth rate of 1.3% (Sognor, *Population Studies*, XVII, 1963). The origins of the 'population revolution' clearly pre-dated the 1780s in areas like these.

The divergency between the demographic experience of rural and industrial areas in the eighteenth century is nowhere more strikingly illustrated than by Professor Chambers in his work on the Vale of Trent (*Economic History Review*, Supplement 3). Whereas the total population of sixty-two agricultural villages in the Trent valley rose by 12.7% between 1743 and 1764, and by a further 38.7% between 1764 and 1801, that of forty nearby industrial villages increased by 47.8% and 96.5% over the same two periods. In the hundred years between the middle of the eighteenth and the middle of the nineteenth centuries, the rate of population growth in rural England, though higher than it had been between 1700 and 1750, continued to lag far behind that of industrial and commercial regions. According to the calculations made by Miss Deane and Professor Cole, while the population of purely rural counties expanded by over 88% between 1751 and 1831, that of industrial and commercial counties rose by 129%.

Throughout the rest of our period, from the middle of the nineteenth century to the end of the 1930s, the general pattern remained very much the same. The population of manufacturing and trading regions continued to expand much more rapidly than

that of agricultural areas. Indeed the rate of population growth
in rural England as a whole slumped well below the level that
had been reached in the years between about 1750 and 1850. A
handful of rural counties actually suffered an absolute decline in
population after the middle of the nineteenth century. The
population of Rutland began to fall more or less steadily from
1851; that of Cornwall from 1861; that of Herefordshire from the
peak attained in 1881. In Wales, the populations of Cardiganshire
and Montgomeryshire fell consistently from 1871 onwards, and of
Merioneth from 1881. In other primarily agricultural areas,
though population did not decline steadily throughout the period,
it nevertheless did fall in the late nineteenth century and thereafter
failed to expand significantly. The population of Westmorland
changed little between 1871 and 1931, while that of Huntingdonshire and Cumberland remained roughly stable from 1891 onwards. In Wales, from varying dates in the late nineteenth century,
the populations of Anglesey, Brecknock, Caernarvon, Pembroke
and Radnor stabilised at well below their former levels. These
cases are, however, exceptions. At least in England, most rural
counties continued to increase in population, albeit very slowly
and even though some of them like Cambridgeshire and Norfolk
suffered a temporary demographic decline in the second half of
the century. But the real growth of English population from the
middle of the nineteenth century took place mainly in industrial
and commercial regions. Of course, there were notable differences
in the pace of population increase from one industrial and commercial area to another. In the half century before 1911 the
greatest increase in regional population occurred in those parts
of the North-East, North-West, West Midlands and South Wales
where the local economy was heavily dependent on thriving basic
industries like coal, iron and steel, cotton and wool. During the
inter-war period, when most of the traditional staple industries
were in a state of chronic depression, the manufacturing and commercial populations growing most rapidly were those in the
Home Counties and the East Midlands (Warwickshire and
Nottinghamshire) where 'new' industries like motor car and
electrical goods-manufacturing were much more bouyant.

The demographic effect of regional variations in the rate of
population growth, themselves the result of marked differences in
the pace and nature of local economic development, has been two-

fold. Firstly, they have caused considerable changes in the geographic distribution of England's population. Secondly, they have led to a drastic alteration in the balance between urban and rural living.

In 1701 the population of the sixteen counties which Deane

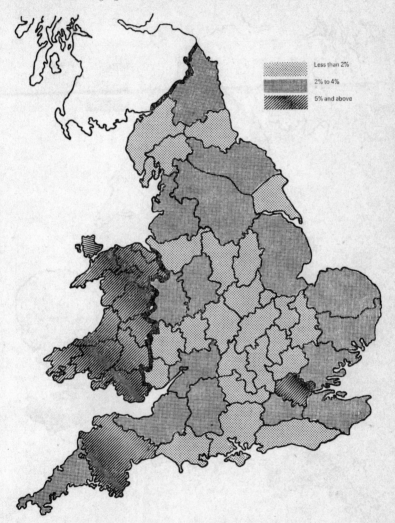

Less than 2%

2% to 4%

5% and above

MAP 1 *The Distribution of the Population of England and Wales in 1701 by County* (as a percentage of total population)

4

and Cole define as rural comprised roughly one-third of the total population of England and Wales; by 1831 slightly above one-quarter, and by 1931 only about one-fifth. On the other hand, that of the group of counties defined by Deane and Cole as primarily industrial and commercial rose from about one-third

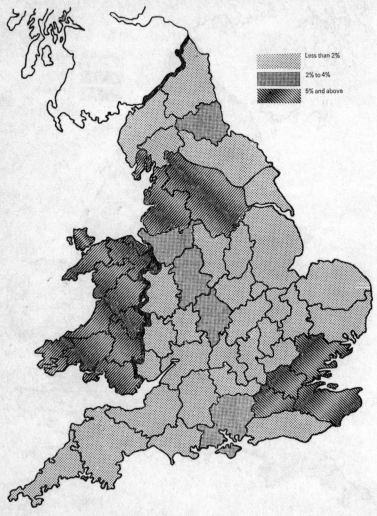

MAP 11 *The Distribution of the Population of England and Wales in 1931 by County* (as a percentage of total population)

of the total population at the beginning of the eighteenth century, to 45% in 1831, and 57% in 1931. Such has been the effect of relatively high rates of population growth in non-agricultural areas since the late seventeenth century.

The two maps which accompany this chapter give a more detailed indication of how the geographical balance of the population has been altered by the forces of economic and demographic growth between 1701 and 1931. In them the population of each county has been represented as a percentage of the total population of England and Wales. In the absence of separate county figures for 1701, Wales had been treated as a single county. The population estimates for 1701 are taken from data provided by Deane and Cole. Those for 1931 are from the census figures for that year quoted by Mitchell and Deane (*Abstract of British Historical Statistics*).

As the maps illustrate, there has been a marked redistribution in the geographic balance of the population since 1701. The distribution of the population between the various counties of England and Wales in the early eighteenth century was much more evenly balanced than it was later to become. Treating Wales and the three Ridings of Yorkshire as separate counties, in 1701 only twenty-four of the forty-three counties each contributed less than 2% to the total population of the country. By 1931 the number had risen to thirty-one. By comparison, the number of relatively populous counties, each having at least 5% of England's total population, increased from three (Wales, Middlesex, Devon) in the early eighteenth century to seven (Wales, Middlesex, Essex, Kent, Surrey, Lancashire, and the West Riding) by the early 1930s. The growing imbalance of residential distribution is accounted for by a decline in the number of counties with between 2% and 5% of the total population (from sixteen in 1701 to five in 1931), and reflects the steady migration of people from agricultural to industrial-commercial areas.

Associated with the geographic redistribution of England's population between 1701 and 1931 has been the tendency for an ever-larger proportion of this population to live in dense urban concentrations, or at least close to them. According to a recent sophisticated analysis of the spread of urbanisation carried out by Friedlander (*Population Studies*, XXIV, 1970), the percentage of the population living in what he defines as 'urbanised regions' (i.e. regions in which less than 10% of all adult males were engaged in agricultural occupations) increased from 25.5% in 1851 to 76.7% in 1931. According to Peter Laslett (*The World we have Lost*) the proportion of population actually living in urban areas rose from perhaps one in every four persons in Gregory King's day, to one in every two by the middle of the nineteenth century, and to over three in every four by the 1930s. At the end of the seventeenth century almost three-quarters of the entire population lived in what King described as villages and hamlets, and most of the so-called urban dwellers outside London lived out their lives in communities with less than a thousand people. As we shall see, quite apart from the enormous changes which urbanisation has wrought on our whole way of life, it has played a vital part in shaping the long-term evolution of fertility, mortality and population growth rates.

2. *Fertility, Mortality and Migration*

Variations in the rate of population increase over time, and between one area and another, are a function either of changes in the rate of natural increase (i.e. in the excess of births over deaths) and/or of alterations in the balance between in- and out-migration. Data on the level of crude birth- and death-rates and on the net balance of migration for England and Wales as a whole are given in Table III and Graphs III and IV below. Readers will note that no attempt has been made to include data for the period before 1841. Prior to the introduction of civil registration in 1837, birth- and death-rate statistics can only be compiled from the baptism and burial totals recorded in the parish registers of the Anglican church. We have already discussed the notorious inadequacy of these as guides to the behaviour of the vital rates, particularly during the late eighteenth and early nineteenth centuries. Despite the exhaustive efforts of Professor Krause and others it is futile to pretend that any reliable study of English birth- and death-rate trends before the 1840s as yet exists. Dr Wrigley's analysis of the Devonshire parish of Colyton based on family reconstitution techniques (*Economic History Review*, XIX, 1966; *Daedalus*, 97, 1968) provides a ray of hope for the future, but it would be most unwise for us to generalise from the demographic experience of one remote rural parish. Elsewhere, especially in growing urban-industrial areas, the pattern of

TABLE III *Birth-rates, Death-rates and Migration in England and Wales, 1841–1938*

Period	Births per thousand population	Deaths per thousand population	Net loss by migration (000)
1841–5	35.2	21.4	−301
1846–50	34.8	23.3	−182
1851–5	35.5	22.7	−787
1856–60	35.5	21.8	−581
1861–5	35.8	22.6	−373
1866–70	35.7	22.4	−434
1871–5	35.7	22.0	−388
1876–80	35.4	20.8	−543
1881–5	33.5	19.4	−706
1886–90	31.4	18.9	−525
1891–5	30.5	18.7	−389
1896–1900	29.3	17.7	−633
1901–05	28.2	16.1	−645
1906–10	26.3	14.7	−577
1911–15	23.6	14.3	−2584
1916–20	20.1	14.4	+1454
1921–25	19.9	12.1	−488
1926–30	16.7	12.1	−227
1931–35	15.0	12.0	+61
1936–38	14.9	12.0	+217

Sources:
Crude birth-rates 1841–45 to 1876–80. D. V. Glass, 'A note on the under-registration of births in Britain in the nineteenth century', *Population Studies*, V, 1, 1951–52. All other statistics calculated from data on the estimated mid-year size of the population, births and birth-rates, deaths and death-rates given by B. R. Mitchell and P. Deane, *Abstract of British Historical Statistics*, Cambridge University Press, 1962, pp. 8–10, 29–30, 34–35, 36–37. For the estimates of net migration 1841–45 to 1876–80 inclusive, the number of births recorded by the Registrar-General and quoted by Mitchell and Deane has been corrected to take account of under-registration, using the correction ratios suggested by D. V. Glass, *Population Studies*, V, 1, 1951–52.

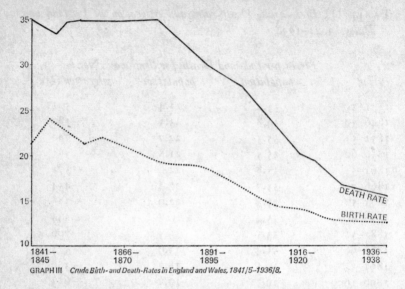

GRAPH III   *Crude Birth- and Death-Rates in England and Wales, 1841/5–1936/8.*

birth-and death-rates was almost certainly very different. Similarly, there is little statistical information on the movement of people into and out of England and Wales before 1841. The normal method of tracing variations in the balance between in- and out-migration (that is, by subtracting the actual increase in population over a given period from the total excess of births over deaths during the same period—the procedure followed in Table III) can only be followed for the period after 1841 when reasonably accurate estimates of total population size and rates of natural increase can be derived from the census and civil registration returns. In any event it has been thought wisest to begin our analysis from the 1840s.

Since they make no allowance for regional and chronological variations in age, sex and marital structures, crude birth- and death-rates are not completely accurate guides to real changes in the levels of fertility and mortality. For the present purpose, however, they serve well enough as a rough indication of the trend in English fertility and mortality since the middle of the nineteenth century.

From the 1840s to the end of the 1870s, crude birth-rates remained high and relatively stable, fluctuating within the narrow range of 34.8 to 35.8 per thousand total population. Thereafter, from the beginning of the 1880s down to 1939, the birth-rate fell continuously with the result that by the period 1936–38 it was 55% lower than the average for the quinquennium 1881–85.

The general pattern was much the same in most other countries of North and West Europe. The level of crude birth-rates began its steady, long-term decline in Sweden from the 1860s. In Belgium, the Netherlands, Denmark, Norway, Finland, Ireland and Scotland (as in England and Wales), the transition to the lower levels of fertility associated with modern industrialised societies got under way from the 1880s. France alone of all Western European countries was different. There, fertility seems to have been falling more or less continuously from as early as the late eighteenth century. But even in France the decline in fertility rates accelerated from the 1880s.

Within England and Wales the start of the long-term decline in rates of fertility almost certainly varied from one social class to another, though a good deal more research is needed to sub-stantiate this point fully. We know that significant differentials in the level of fertility between the various social classes and from one part of the country to another long pre-dated the 1880s. John Graunt, the founding father of English demographic science in the seventeenth century, commented on the relative infertility of urban marriages and blamed the evil effects of 'smoaks, stinks and close air' and of 'anxieties of the mind' on the fecundity of urban businessmen (*Natural and Political Observations* . . ., 5th ed., London, 1676). His near contemporary, Charles Davenant, also wrote of the poor fertility of urban marriages which he explained as the result of the 'greater luxury and intemperance' and the 'unhealthfulness of the coal smoke' in urban areas (*Discourses on the Public Revenues and on the Trade of England*, 2 vols., 1698). In a recent article, Loschky and Krier have demonstrated that average completed family size among gentry, farmer, craftsman and tradesman classes in eighteenth-century Lancashire was noticeably smaller than that among the labouring population (*Journal of Economic History*, XXIX, 1969). For a somewhat later period, using data from the 1911 fertility census, Judah Matras has revealed the marked fertility differentials which already existed between the marriages of the principal social classes of England and Wales during the three or four decades before 1880 (*Population Studies*, XIX, 1965). For at least one social group in which reproduction rates were relatively low in the mid-nineteenth century, the British peerage, the long-run decline in fertility had begun as early as the opening of the century, though it did accelerate during the 1880s (T. Hollingsworth, *The Demography of the British Peerage*). What we do not yet know is whether the same early decline in fertility was common to all those upper- and middle-class groups whose reproductive norms were already below average by 1880. This remains to be tested. In the meantime, while allowing that for England and Wales as a whole the secular fall in fertility only began from the 1880s, we must also recognise the probability that in certain social classes it had begun rather earlier.

Once under way after 1880, the pace at which the level of fertility declined varied greatly from one social group to another. Before the outbreak of the First World War it was most pronounced among families in the upper, middle, retired and private income sections of the population, somewhat less dramatic among those of skilled, semi-skilled and textile workers, and least obvious of all within the social classes represented by unskilled industrial workers, miners, and agricultural labourers. In other words, during the initial phase of the transition to lower fertility, the socio-occupational differentials in rates of fertility which already existed actually widened. In the period between the world wars, on the other hand, this pattern was reversed. The sharpest fall in fertility now occurred within those social classes which at the beginning of the inter-war period had had the highest birth-rates. However, although there was some narrowing of social class fertility differentials during the 1920s and 1930s, substantial differences still remained. Thus, in 1939, the lowest rates of fertility were to be found in social classes I, II and X (professional and administrative personnel, employers and clerks), and the highest in social classes V, VII, VIII (unskilled industrial workers, miners, and agricultural labourers), whilst the fertility rates of groups VI, XI, XII (textile workers, shop assistants, personal service employees, foremen) and of groups IV, IX, XIII (semi-skilled manual workers, farmers, other ranks in the police and armed forces) lay somewhere between the two extremes (Hopkin and Hajnal, *Population Studies*, I, 1947).

Crude death-rates changed little in England and Wales during the three decades between 1841 and 1870. Thereafter, apart from the minor and temporary setback in the quinquennium 1916–20, they fell continuously and fairly regularly. Significantly, however, the long-term decline in mortality since the late nineteenth century has proceeded much more slowly than that of fertility. As a result, the total population of England and Wales during the inter-war period increased considerably less rapidly than it had done at any stage since the middle of the eighteenth century.

The use of crude death-rates to illustrate mortality trends tends to obscure important differences in the onset of the secular fall in mortality by age-group. Mortality rates in the age-groups between 5 and 34 years began their continuous decline from at least as early as the middle of the 1840s, and accelerated from the late 1860s and 1870s. Those in the age-group 35–44 years began to fall from the mid-1870s; those for the ages between 45 and 74 years only from the middle of the 1890s. Infant death rates (that is, the number of deaths between the ages 0 and 1 year per thousand live births) remained unchanged from 1841 to 1870, then fell slightly during the 1870s and 1880s, rose sharply in the last decade of the century and only began their long-term decline from the period 1901–10. The overall result of this complex pattern of declining mortality rates was a steady improvement in the average expectation of life. Males and females born between 1838 and 1854 could expect to live on average 39.9 and 41.9 years respectively. For those born in the period 1901–12 average life expectancy at birth had risen to 51.5 and 55.4 years, and for the cohort born between 1930 and 1932 to 58.7 and 62.9 years.

Once again it is worth stressing that the general pattern of English mortality experience since the middle of the nineteenth century was very similar to that observed elsewhere in Western Europe, though there were slight variations from one country to another in the date at which mortality began its transition to lower levels. The continuous decline in crude death-rates in Belgium and the Netherlands began from at least as early as the 1840s, in Denmark and Sweden from the 1860s, in Finland, France and Scotland (like England and Wales) from about the 1870s, and in Norway from the 1890s.

The use of crude death-rates to illustrate the evolution of mortality also tends to obscure the existence of substantial variations in the rate of mortality between the different social classes. Most noticeable were the social class differentials which existed in the levels of infant mortality. According to data available for 1911, with the exception of agricultural labourers and textile workers (the former with abnormally low, and the latter with abnormally high infant death-rates), there was a close, positive correlation between socio-occupational class variations in the levels of fertility and infant mortality: social groups with relatively low rates of fertility were also those blessed by a lower than average rate of infant mortality, whilst social groups with higher fertility norms suffered very much severer death-rates in infancy. Significant infant mortality differentials by social class still existed in the 1930s. Indeed, according to evidence assembled by Professor Titmuss, they may actually have widened in the course of the inter-war period. Thus, the rate of infant mortality among upper- and middle-class families fell from 61% of the average for all classes in 1911 to 53% in 1930–32. By contrast, the rate of mortality among families of the unskilled labouring population rose slightly from 122% of the average for all classes in 1911 to 125% in 1930–32 (R. M. Titmuss, *Birth, Poverty and Wealth*).

High rates of population growth were maintained throughout the second half of the nineteenth and early twentieth centuries despite a heavy net loss of people by migration overseas. Over the whole period 1841–1939, when the total population of England and Wales rose from 15.9 to 41.5 million, a further 8.6 million— over one-third of the actual increase in population between the two dates—emigrated.

The net movement of people overseas varied considerably from one period to another. If we exclude the decade of the First World War when 'normal' migration patterns were disturbed by the effects of conscription and demobilisation, the greatest losses occurred during the 1850s, especially from 1851 to 1855; during the period from the middle of the 1870s to the end of the 1880s, particularly between 1881 and 1885; and from the mid-1890s to about 1910. The net drain of people overseas was much less serious during the years 1841–50, 1861–75, 1891–95, and 1921–30. For the first time, in the 1930s, the population of England and Wales actually gained on the net balance of migration, when over a quarter of a million more people came into the country than left it. The century-long drain of Englishmen going overseas had

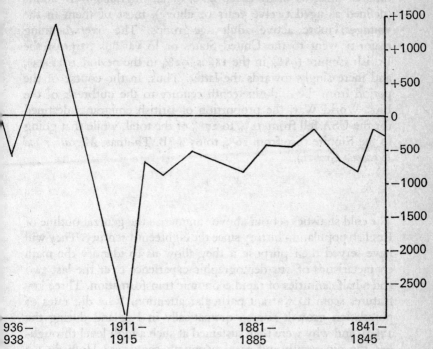

936–	1911–	1881–	1841–
938	1915	1885	1845

APH IV   *Net Gain or Loss by Overseas Migration in England and Wales by sub-periods,*

at last come to an end. Clearly, although emigration was partly responsible for the slight fall in the pace of English population growth in the late nineteenth and early twentieth centuries, the sharp downturn in rates of population increase during the inter-war period was not related to any further rise in the balance of emigrants over immigrants.

For a more detailed discussion of the composition and direction of migration from Britain we must turn to Professor Thomas's analysis of nineteenth- and twentieth-century passenger lists, though it should be stressed that these do not deal with the movement of people between Britain and Europe. Of all emigrants leaving British ports for countries outside Europe before the outbreak of the First World War, six out of every ten were males, a significant and rising proportion of whom could be classified as professional and skilled men. Although varying somewhat from time to time, as many as 80–90% of all migrants were adults (defined as aged twelve years or above), most of them in the younger, more active adult age-groups. The overwhelming majority went to the United States or to various parts of the British Empire (98% in the 1860s, 92% in the period 1911–13), and increasingly towards the latter. Thus, in the course of the period from the mid-nineteenth century to the outbreak of the First World War, the proportion of British emigrants destined for the USA fell from 72% to 27% of the total, while that going to the Empire rose from 26% to 65% (B. Thomas, *Migration and Economic Growth*).

* * *

The cold statistics set out above summarise the general outline of English population history since the eighteenth century. They will have served their purpose if they allow us to identify the main characteristics of our demographic experience over the last two and a half centuries of rapid economic transformation. Three key features seem to warrant particular attention. Why did rates of population growth rise so dramatically in England during the 1780s, and why were they sustained at such a high level throughout the nineteenth and early twentieth centuries? How do we account for the sudden deceleration in the pace of population increase during the period between the two world wars? What were the forces which were responsible for the phenomenal surge in emigration in the sixty years or so after the middle of the nineteenth century, and how do we explain the marked short-run variations which occurred in the rate of emigration within this period?

These are the questions upon which historical demographers have lavished most of their attention in recent years. We will consider them in Chapters III and IV below. But the study of demography is important to the historian not only because he is interested in identifying the forces which shape population trends but also because the population variable itself exerts its own powerful influence on the character of economic, social and political development. In the last two chapters of this short volume we must try to show how the 'population revolution', the transition to lower rates of population growth in the twentieth century, and the phenomenon of mass overseas migration have each contributed to the changes which have taken place in the economic and social structure of England since the early days of the Industrial Revolution.

FURTHER READING

Books and Monographs

A. Armengaud, 'Population in Europe, 1700-1914', in C. M. Cipolla (ed.), *The Fontana Economic History of Europe*, Vol. III, Chapter I, London and Glasgow, 1970.

J. D. Chambers, *The Vale of Trent, 1670-1800, Economic History Review*, Supplement 3, 1957.

P. Deane and W. A. Cole, *British Economic Growth, 1688-1959*, 2nd ed., Cambridge University Press, 1967.

D. V. Glass and E. Grebenik, 'World population 1800-1950', in H. J. Habbakkuk and M. Postan (eds.), *The Cambridge Economic History of Europe*, Vol. VI, Part I, Cambridge University Press, 1967.

J. W. Innes, *Class Fertility Trends in England and Wales, 1876-1934*, Princeton University Press, Princeton, 1938.

B. Thomas, *Migration and Economic Growth. A study of Great Britain and the Atlantic Economy*, Cambridge University Press, 1954.

R. M. Titmuss, *Birth, Poverty and Wealth*, London, 1943.

Articles

N. H. Carrier, 'An examination of generation fertility in England and Wales', *Population Studies*, IX, 1955.

J. W. B. Douglas, 'Social class differences in health and survival', *Population Studies*, V, 1, 1951.

D. E. C. Eversley, 'A survey of population in an area of Worcestershire from 1660 to 1850', *Population Studies*, X, 1957.

D. V. Glass, 'Gregory King's estimate of the population of England and Wales, 1695', *Population Studies*, II, 1950.

W. A. B. Hopkin and J. Hajnal, 'Analysis of births in England and Wales, 1939, by father's occupation', Part I, *Population Studies*, I, 2, 1947.

J. T. Krause, 'Changes in English fertility and mortality, 1781–1850', *Economic History Review*, XI, 1, 1958.

W. P. D. Logan, 'Mortality in England and Wales from 1848–1947', *Population Studies*, IV, 2, 1950.

J. Matras, 'Social strategies of family formation. Data for British female cohorts born 1831–1906', *Population Studies*, XIX, 2, 1965.

S. Peller, 'Mortality past and future', *Population Studies*, I, 4, 1948.

G. Rowntree and R. M. Pierce, 'Birth control in Britain. Part I. Attitudes and practices among persons married since World War I', *Population Studies*, XV, 1961–62.

S. Sogner, 'Aspects of the demographic situation in seventeen parishes in Shropshire', 1711–60, *Population Studies*, XVIII, 1963.

G. S. L. Tucker, 'English pre-industrial population trends', *Economic History Review*, XVI, 2, 1965.

E. A. Wrigley, 'Family limitation in pre-industrial England', *Economic History Review*, XIX, 1, 1966.

E. A. Wrigley, 'Mortality in pre-industrial England', *Daedalus*, 97, 2, 1968.

3. The 'Population Revolution'

Between 1086, the date of *Domesday Book*, and 1781 the population of England and Wales rose slowly and spasmodically from perhaps 1.2 to 7.5 million—a mere six to sevenfold increase in almost seven hundred years. The trouble was that the long periods of relatively rapid population growth (from the eleventh to the end of the thirteenth, and from the early sixteenth to the mid-seventeenth centuries) were countered by almost equally long periods of demographic stagnation and at times even of actual decline (from the early fourteenth to the late fifteenth, and from the mid-seventeenth to the mid-eighteenth centuries), with the result that overall rates of population increase were sharply curtailed.

From 1781 to 1939, on the other hand, the population of England and Wales rose from 7.5 to 41.5 million—a five to sixfold increase in the space of only one hundred and sixty years. This notable acceleration in the pace of population growth in modern times is what historical demographers mean by the term 'population revolution'. In this chapter we will try to account for it.

* * *

Man has always had some influence over his own rate of increase. Even among the most primitive peoples levels of mortality were at least partly determined by the economic, social and political environment which men had fashioned for themselves. The prevalence of war or peace, the standards of personal and public health, the ease with which agriculture could meet the demand for food and raw materials, the efficiency of the transport system in distributing foodstuffs—all these and many more besides depend partly on human activity and ingenuity, and from time immemorial all have exerted their influence on the behaviour of mortality rates. Periodic variations in the levels of fertility too have always owed something to deliberate human actions: even in the most backward societies they mirrored in part man's own conscious decisions to raise or lower his age at, or frequency of, marriage, or to extend or reduce the frequency of abortion, infanticide or rudimentary birth-control practices.

However, when full allowance has been made for the rôle of the human agent, it remains true that the pattern of population growth in all pre-modern societies was basically a function of factors which lay well outside the sphere of human control and responsibility. Until recently, the evolution of both mortality and fertility, and hence the pace of population growth, was in the main determined by what we might call uncontrollable, autonomous 'natural forces'—by variations in climatic conditions, in the natural severity of disease virus or in the resistance of the human host towards disease, and even in the ecology of disease-carrying animal and rodent populations. In primitive societies, the abundance of the food harvest was closely dependent on fluctuations in climate, much more so than it is in the modern world with its advantages of superior agricultural techniques, wider and more varied sources of food supply and sophisticated storage facilities; and in communities where the standards of income and nutrition were both relatively low, variations in harvest yield were more likely to have immediate and dramatic effects on the levels of mortality and fertility. Amongst populations which lacked the protection afforded by modern medical and public health services any autonomous alteration in the virulence of epidemic viruses or in human resistance towards them could work much more freely on birth- and death-rates than they do nowadays when their worst effects can be kept under control. Put simply, the long-term rate of population growth in pre-industrial England was low primarily because average levels of mortality remained relatively high: and mortality rates were high because man had not yet learnt how to control the workings of the 'forces of nature'.

At first glance the explanation for the 'take-off' in rates of population growth which accompanied the arrival of modern industrial society seems perfectly straightforward. What happened was that the various 'natural forces' which until then had worked largely unhindered to keep the death-rate high were finally brought under human control. Better methods of agricultural production at home, the discovery and development of new overseas sources of food supply, and the steady rise in average real incomes associated with the cumulative process of industrialisation and economic growth combined together to eliminate once and for all the danger of severe food shortages, and to raise the standards of per capita food output and diet to such a level that the age-old link between malnutrition and the spread of fatal disease largely disappeared. At the same time, the adoption of improved medical, public health and social service facilities was launching its own more direct attack on the various conditions which from time immemorial had been responsible for keeping death-rates high. As a result of man's greater control over the workings of his natural environment, the rate of mortality declined, and the pace of population growth quickened. It is significant that when the rate of population growth fell in the period between the two world wars it did so not because mortality rose but simply because of a rational, conscious human decision to reduce the rates of reproduction.

As an explanation for the 'population revolution' in its later stages—that is, from the middle of the nineteenth to the second decade of the twentieth century, when the rate of demographic increase fell—this interpretation is amply supported by the known facts. The maintenance of high rates of population growth through the half century or so prior to the outbreak of the First World War was clearly the result of falling mortality, and not rising fertility: and death-rates fell after 1850 because rising standards of nutrition, improved methods of water supply and refuse disposal, the growing concern for personal cleanliness and child welfare, and the spread of vaccination began to cut back on the number of deaths caused by infectious diseases like tuberculosis, typhus, typhoid, cholera and smallpox.

In view of the evidence available one wonders, however, whether the same explanation can be applied to the initial phase of population 'take-off' in the period between 1780 and 1850. Was the first stage of the 'population revolution' triggered-off by falling mortality? Or was it instead due to rising fertility? If a decline in death-rates *was* the primary variable at work, how do we account for the fact that mortality fell? Was it because the benefits which were ultimately to accrue from industrialisation were already available in 1780? In other words, were relatively high rates of population growth between 1780 and 1850, like

those after 1850, really due to increasing human control over the
demographic effects of the exogenous forces of nature? Or must
we look elsewhere for our explanation? After all, many historians
believe that the average standards of life actually deteriorated
during the period of early industrial 'take-off', and many others
believe that there was little improvement in these standards
before the mid-nineteenth century. If they are correct (and the
facts are still hotly debated) we cannot assume that the rise in the
rate of population growth before 1850 was the result of the same
factors which were operative after 1850. Could, perhaps, the early
demographic 'take-off' have stemmed from other aspects of
human activity—say, for instance, an increasing demand for
labour and the stimulus which this gave to fertility? Or could it
simply have been due to a natural reduction in the frequency and
severity of fatal disease—a reduction which was quite independent of any improvements or innovations made by man?
Clearly, only a very close look at the evidence that is available
will help us to decide. It is with the vexing period 1780–1850
that the rest of this chapter will be concerned.

*   *   *

As Dr Eversley has pointed out (*Population Studies*, X, 1957), the
'take-off' in the rate of English population growth after 1780 was
in part simply the result of the demographic experience of preceding generations. In pre-modern societies periods of demographic 'crisis', when the population stagnated or declined in
size, were invariably followed by periods of relatively high rates
of population increase; partly because the size of the 'post-crisis'
population was small relative to the number of economic opportunities, making it easier for people to marry earlier and have
larger families; partly because the surviving population was
particularly healthy and robust, and therefore less prone to fatal
illness; perhaps also because the disease viruses had spent much
of their previous force. Thus, the years of demographic stagnation
in England between the 1720s and the 1740s, when death-rates
were high and marriage- and birth-rates unusually low, were
succeeded by a phase of demographic recovery between the 1750s
and the 1770s, during which mortality stabilised at lower levels
and both nuptiality and fertility rates rose substantially. Not only

were more children born in the thirty years after 1750, but a relatively high proportion of them survived into adulthood, ultimately to become parents themselves. When this 'bulge-generation' reached maturity in the last quarter of the century it provided its own positive stimulus to the marriage- and birth-rates of the period and helped to create a demographic age-structure which, by virtue of the abnormally large percentage of young adults it contained, was peculiarly favourable to low rates of mortality.

No one doubts the validity of this argument, though its relative significance has never been properly quantified. By itself, how-ever, the 'bulge-generation' thesis cannot account for more than a small part of the upturn in the rate of population increase which occurred after 1780. By common consent, the principal explana-tions of the early 'population revolution' must lie elsewhere.

For convenience' sake, the explanations which recur most frequently can be classified into two broad groups: in the first, those which see the early 'population revolution' as in one way or another the logical outcome of a rapidly changing and expanding economy: in the second, those which regard it as the consequence of various improvements made in the techniques and practices of medicine. Each of these two broad groups embraces a number of different possibilities.

1. *The Economic Case*

Of all the 'economic' interpretations of population 'take-off', the easiest to understand are those which see the upturn in rates of population growth after 1780 as the simple result of a rise in average standards of life made possible by rapid economic progress. Implicitly if not explicitly, most writers on the subject have equated the 'population revolution' with some immediate and recognisable improvement in the standards of living brought about by the Industrial and Agricultural Revolutions of the late eighteenth and early nineteenth centuries. The more optimistic of them see it as the consequence of an *all-round* improvement in levels of popular welfare. Slicher von Bath (*An Agrarian History of Western Europe*), for example, believes that the various eighteenth- and early nineteenth-century developments in industry, agricul-ture and transport led to an immediate rise in the level of per capita real incomes, in the standards of nutrition, and in what he somewhat vaguely defines as the level of 'general comfort'. Other scholars who can be grouped in the same broad category are, however, rather more selective of the benefits which accrued from early industrial, commercial and agricultural expansion. W. L. Langer (*American Historical Review*, LXIX, 1963), for example, places his emphasis solely on the rise in nutritional standards caused by the widespread adoption of the potato in the diet of the common man. Reinhard and Armengaud (*Histoire générale de la population mondiale*) also consider dietary improvements to be the key to population 'take-off', but see them as the result of an all-round improvement in methods of agricultural production, and of the effects of transport innovations in combating the old problem of regional food shortages. A similar line has recently been taken by Professor McKeown and his colleagues. 'It is concluded that the reduction of mortality and the rise of population in the eighteenth and early nineteenth centuries was probably due to a significant increase in food supplies, which spread throughout Europe from the seventeenth century' (T. McKeown, R. G. Brown, R. G. Record, *Population Studies*, XXVI, 1972). Other writers like Professor Chambers (*The Workshop of the World*, London, 1961) concentrate instead on the importance of rising standards of personal hygiene brought about by the greater availability and more extensive use of cheap washable cotton clothes, soap, pottery, ironware utensils. Yet others, like McKeown and Brown in an earlier article (*Population Studies*, IX, 1955) prefer to stress the rôle of improved environmental and public health conditions—better housing with the more general use of bricks and tiles, and better methods of water-supply, sewerage and refuse disposal. But whatever the individual emphasis might be, common to all the above writers is the belief that in one way or another standards of life rose in the late eighteenth and early nineteenth centuries, and it was this which generated the 'take-off' in rates of population growth.

The other possible 'economic' explanations of the early 'population revolution' are more difficult to understand, perhaps because we are naturally reluctant to believe that the upturn in rates of population growth could have been achieved in any other way than by some positive improvement in the conditions of life. Yet we must allow for the possibility that certain characteristics of the 'new' industrial economy may have led to higher rates of population growth despite the fact that there was no simultaneous rise in the average levels of real wages, standards of diet, or personal and public health. Indeed it is conceivable that the rate of demographic increase reached its peak in the early nineteenth century at precisely the time when the standards of living were actually declining.

Consider, for instance, the possible effects on population of an increase in the aggregate demand for labour. The enormous expansion of factory, and to a certain extent handicraft, industry during the late eighteenth and early nineteenth centuries coupled with the spread of new, labour-intensive methods of production in the agricultural sector of the economy led to an almost insatiable demand for both adult and child labour, and caused a substantial rise in individual and family money (but not necessarily real) earnings. At the same time certain changes in the nature of industrial and agricultural employment provided a further impetus to the rise in money incomes. In industry, the spread of factory techniques of mass production meant that much of the additional demand for labour was for unskilled and semi-skilled workers rather than for highly trained craftsmen. As the emphasis on industrial craftsmanship decreased, the need for workers to serve long periods of poorly-paid apprenticeship also decreased, with the result that the money earnings of young adults rose substantially. In agriculture, the gradual decline in the practice of 'living-in', whereby agricultural labourers lodged in the home of their employer, gave many rural labourers an independence (or, at least, a *sense* of independence) which they had previously lacked. Conceivably, until the agricultural depression of the post-Napoleonic war years anyway, they used this new-found 'freedom' to seek out, and bargain for, higher money-wages. The suggestion is that rising money wages alone could have caused an upturn in rates of population growth even though the levels of real wages and the conditions of life generally were themselves deteriorating. Provided that real incomes, dietary, health and hygiene standards did not fall too far (and thus cause a rise in mortality), an increase in money earnings might have triggered off higher rates of population growth through the encouragement it gave to earlier marriage and higher rates of marital fertility.

But how could this happen? After all, under normal circumstances, people are quite capable of appreciating that rising *money* wages do not necessarily mean rising *real* wages, and that early marriage and additional children usually entail a considerable material sacrifice. If, as many writers claim, real wages were falling in the early nineteenth century despite the rise in money incomes, why did the population not counter this by delaying marriage and limiting its fertility? Why instead did people marry ever earlier and bear ever larger numbers of children? The answer must lie in the fact that the late eighteenth and early nineteenth centuries was a far from normal period. The great and sudden increase in the opportunities for regular employment for both men and women, the possibility of earning relatively high money wages in young adult age-groups, above all the apparently limitless demand for child labour combined to foster the wide-spread belief that early marriage and larger families did not result in serious material sacrifices—indeed, that they offered the chance for positive material gain. Even that most sophisticated of contemporary observers, Arthur Young, was convinced of this.

Why have the inhabitants of Birmingham increased from 23,000 in 1750 to 30,000 in 1770? Certainly because a pro-portional increase of employment has taken place. Wherever there is a demand for hands, there they will abound: this demand is but another word for ease of subsistence, which operates in the same manner . . . as the plenty of land in the back country of America. Marriages abound there, because children are no burthen—they abound in Birmingham for the same reason, as every child as soon as it can use its hands, can maintain itself, and the father and mother need never to want employment, that is, income— and—support. Thus where employment increases (Birmingham) the people increase: and where employment does not increase, (Col-chester) the people do not increase . . . Away my boys—get children, they are worth more than ever they were (A. Young, *Political Arithmetic*, London, 1774).

It matters little that Arthur Young, and the many others who thought like him, was quite wrong. No doubt the net costs of raising children did decline as the opportunities for child labour increased, but it is unlikely that a child's earnings ever covered more than a part of the costs of his upbringing. High fertility

certainly pauperised many families who would otherwise have
been very much better off. The salient point is, however, that
most people failed to realise this. For much of the eighteenth
and early nineteenth centuries the populations of manufacturing
regions seem to have assumed that the sudden upsurge in employment opportunities for themselves and their children (and the
rise in money incomes which resulted from it) was a passport to
higher real standards of life. They behaved as if convinced that
the richest material rewards which the new industrial society had
to offer went to those who married the earliest and bore the
largest number of children. How else can we explain the high
marriage- and birth-rates prevailing in urban-industrial areas?
How else can we account for the endless stream of young men
and women who poured into the rapidly expanding manufacturing
towns? As more and more young people crowded into manufacturing regions, they helped to create those peculiarly youthful
age-structures which were characteristic of the early urban-
industrial communities and which acted as a further incentive to
early marriage and higher rates of marital fertility among the
populations of such areas. By the late eighteenth century the proportion of England's population living in manufacturing districts
was large enough for the effects of industrialisation on marriage
and fertility to be reflected in national average marriage- and
birth-rate trends. The result was that the pace of English population growth quickened.

Finally within the context of potential 'economic' explanations
of population 'take-off', we are also asked to consider the possible
demographic effects of the so-called Speenhamland system of poor
relief, particularly as it was applied during the Napoleonic war
years when rates of relief were at their most generous. Some time
ago, Professor Krause (*Economic History Review*, XI, 1958), taking
his cue from a long line of distinguished contemporary commen-
tators like the Reverend Thomas Malthus, set out the argument
that the introduction of a sliding scale of poor relief after 1795,
in which the amount of relief varied directly both with the price
of bread and the size of family, acted as a 'bounty on population',
and greatly stimulated rates of population growth in those parts
of rural England where it was widely adopted. Because farmers
preferred to hire married rather than unmarried men, in their
efforts to keep the burden of local poor rates down, Speenhamland

worked in favour of early marriage and strongly discouraged celibacy. Because allowances in aid of wages eased the financial burdens which additional children imposed on their parents, it also led to higher rates of marital fertility. It is difficult to decide whether we are meant to assume from this that the Speenhamland system led to earlier marriages and higher birth-rates by actually raising the level of real wages and general standards of comfort among those populations to whom it was widely applied. In view of the undoubted distress in Speenhamland areas during the early nineteenth century this would be an extremely difficult proposition to sustain. Perhaps all that we are meant to assume is that the new and more liberal form of poor relief adopted after 1795 simply cushioned rural populations against the worst effects of unemployment and rising food prices by guaranteeing a basic 'living' income, and that the sense of security which this instilled was enough to induce agricultural labourers to give freer rein to their natural desires to marry early and have large numbers of children.

Whether the amounts of relief given by parish poor law overseers under the Speenhamland system really were sufficiently generous to have had such demographic effects was a question subsequently taken up by Mark Blaug, one of Professor Krause's earliest critics (*Journal of Economic History*, XXIII, 1963). According to Blaug, if Speenhamland stimulated the rate of population growth at all (and he is admittedly somewhat sceptical about this), it did so not through any incentive it might have given to marriage and fertility but rather through the beneficial effects it might have had on the level of mortality. Thus, although the amounts of relief were too small to act as a stimulus in favour of earlier marriage and higher rates of marital fertility, they may have been large enough to have brought about a slight rise in standards of diet, thereby reducing the number of deaths resulting directly or indirectly from undernourishment and malnutrition. Both Krause and Blaug are, however, agreed that whatever the demographic mechanisms involved, whether rising fertility or falling mortality, the Speenhamland system of poor relief was practised over a sufficiently wide area for it to have had some influence on the rates of population increase in rural England, and indeed on those for England and Wales as a whole. Even as late as 1824, long after Speenhamland had passed its peak, it was still being fairly extensively applied in at least sixteen rural counties.

These, then, are the three principal 'economic' explanations of English population 'take-off' in its initial phase between 1780 and 1850: that, as in the second half of the nineteenth and early twentieth centuries, it was due to falling mortality brought about by a general improvement in the average standards of life; that it was instead, a consequence of the enormous increase in the demand for labour and of a rise in money wages, working through the medium of rising fertility; that, at least in parts of rural England and particularly between 1795 and 1820, it owed a good deal to the adoption of a more liberal system of poor relief which stimulated higher rates of population growth either by encouraging an increase in fertility or by contributing to a decline in mortality.

To what extent does the available evidence support each of these 'economic' interpretations?

How far was the 'take-off' in rates of English population growth between 1780 and 1850 the result of a noticeable improvement in the general conditions of life brought about by the Industrial and Agricultural Revolutions of the period? Can we, in other words, equate the early 'population revolution' with rising real wages, more adequate diets, or improved standards of public health and personal hygiene?

If there is any unanimity at all in the scholarly debate on working-class real wage trends during the period 1780–1850 it relates to the three decades between 1790 and 1820. Historians are generally agreed that the economic dislocations of the war and immediate post-war years, worsening terms of trade, and a succession of bad harvests at a time when population was growing rapidly, all combined to cause some (unmeasured) decline in the level of per capita real incomes during the thirty years or so after 1790. Yet it was precisely during this period that the rate of population increase was at its most rapid, reaching a peak in the sadly-troubled decade 1811–1820. At some (ill-defined) stage between 1821 and 1850 the level of real wages stabilised, and towards the end of the period real wages may even have begun to rise slightly. Despite this, the rate of population growth actually fell slightly from the peak that had been attained during the 1810s. On the face of it, therefore, there is nothing to suggest that the secular trends in real wages and population moved in unison during the period 1790–1850, and consequently no reason to suppose that the 'take-off' in population from the 1780s was the result of a simultaneous and consistent rise in average per capita real incomes.

Much the same sort of conclusion must be drawn for the contribution made by standards of diet, public health and personal hygiene. Dietary standards are, of course, to a large extent determined by the level of real wages. When real incomes fell during the war and immediate post-war years, the per capita consumption of tea, sugar, meat, fruit and vegetables, bread and so on also fell. Although the nutritional content of popular diets may have improved thereafter, there is no reason to suppose that any significant improvement occurred before at least the middle of the nineteenth century, despite the widespread cultivation of 'new' food crops like the potato. Until the availability of cheap foodstuffs from the New World in the later part of the century, total stocks of basic good supplies barely did more than keep pace with a rapidly growing population. The evidence which we have on conditions of public health is likewise fairly conclusive. The sporadic campaign waged by the pioneer sanitary reformers of the late eighteenth and early nineteenth centuries had only a temporary and geographically very limited effect. Until the 1840s it lacked the necessary public support to achieve anything significant. Indeed, rather than environmental conditions improving during the first half of the nineteenth century, it is likely that for large sections of the population they deteriorated still further as the rapid concentration of people into densely crowded urban-industrial areas magnified the age-old problems of drainage, water-supply and housing. Faced with problems of such novel magnitude the campaign for sanitary reform made little real headway until very much later in the century. On the question of personal hygiene standards, the evidence is much less satisfactory and far less conclusive. Whatever the *potential* effects of the greater output of cotton clothes, soap, pottery etc. on standards of personal cleanliness, we know very little about their *actual* effects. More information on the way such articles were distributed among the various social groups of the population and about the use to which they were put is needed before we can come to any conclusion. Were, for example, the new industrial products consumed mainly by the middle-classes? Was soap used for domestic or for industrial purposes? Were cotton garments washed frequently enough to keep them clean? In any case, even if some slight improvement in the standards of human hygiene did occur (and this has still to be demonstrated), its beneficial effects on the levels of mortality may have been completely offset by the deterioration of public health conditions among the populations of urban-industrial regions.

There is, then, no real evidence to support the view that the early 'take-off' in rates of English population growth between 1780 and 1850 was the result of either rising real per capita incomes, more adequate diets, or improving standards of public health and personal cleanliness. On the contrary, such evidence as we possess suggests quite the opposite. Population first 'took-off' in the period between 1780 and 1820 despite some deterioration in real wage, nutrition and environmental standards.

This conclusion should not, however, be taken to imply that the 'conditions of life' had no part to play in the initial stages of the English 'population revolution'. If only in a negative sense they were extremely significant. Had living standards fallen drastically, high rates of population increase would inevitably have been checked, either by the imposition of deliberate controls on fertility or, more probably, by a rise in death-rates. Fortunately, because the economy grew almost as quickly as population, the standards of real wages, nutrition, public health and personal hygiene for most people always remained above the basic levels at which outbreaks of fatal disease become endemic. Because average living conditions never declined seriously, there was no danger that the 'population revolution' would be brought to an abrupt halt by rapidly rising death-rates (or by fertility limitation) as happened in contemporary Ireland. This is, of course, a very different interpretation of the part played by the 'standards of life' in the early population 'take-off' from that which sees the 'population revolution' as the result of a positive rise in general living conditions. It is, however, the one which best fits the known facts.

A more acceptable explanation of early English demographic 'take-off' is that which sees it as the consequence of rising fertility brought about by an increase in the demand for labour (particularly that of children) and higher money wages. Given man's natural desire to marry and reproduce, the slight fall in the net costs of raising a child which resulted from the growth of employment opportunities was quite sufficient to stimulate earlier marriage and higher rates of marital fertility among the populations of urban-industrial areas, even though in real terms industrialisation did not lead to an immediate improvement in overall standards of life. Whatever our reservations about the impressionistic opinions of contemporary observers like Arthur Young or about the weaknesses of the statistical data assembled by recent scholars like Professor Chambers (*The Vale of Trent*) and Miss Deane and Professor Cole (*British Economic Growth 1688–1959*), two conclusions are inescapable.

Firstly, regional variations in the level of fertility were closely linked to regional differences in the pace and extent of industrial development. As Professor Chambers has shown, in the Vale of Trent throughout the second half of the eighteenth century, the crude rates of baptism and marriage, and the average number of baptisms per marriage, were consistently higher in industrial than in agricultural villages. According to Deane and Cole crude birth-rates in the industrialising counties of North-Western England averaged 39.6 in 1751–80, 39.8 in 1781–1800 and 38.5 in 1801–30. By comparison those in the agricultural counties of Southern England were noticeably lower (36.6, 37.1 and 37.2 respectively). If, as seems likely, the underregistration of births in the parish registers of the Anglican church was relatively more serious in manufacturing areas, then, in reality, the difference between the fertility rates of industrial and agricultural populations was probably even more striking than these figures suggest. Without doubt, people living near to the main centres of industrial growth had higher rates of reproduction than those living elsewhere.

Secondly, by the late eighteenth century anyway, the proportion of the total population living in or near to manufacturing districts was large enough for the effects of industrialisation on the fertility of industrial communities to show in the behaviour of national average birth-rates. According to Dr Armstrong (*Annales de Demographie Historique*, 1965) 23.6% of the total labour-force in 1789 was engaged in manufacturing, mining and other industrial occupations. By 1821 the proportion had risen to 38.4%, and by 1851 to 42.9%. *If* Professor Krause is correct in arguing that

English birth-rates rose in the period from the 1780s to the 1810s the basic explanation might well be the rapid transfer of people from agricultural into manufacturing occupations. *If* he is also right in believing that national birth-rates fell somewhat between the 1810s and the 1840s the root cause may be the relatively slow rate at which manufacturing industry absorbed rural labour during the later years of our period, together with the gradual introduction of statutory legislation against child employment.

How far the rise in fertility among the populations of industrial regions was supplemented by increasing birth-rates in purely rural, agricultural communities is more difficult to determine. There is no conclusive evidence on the demographic effects of either the growing demand for agricultural labour or of the Speenhamland system of poor relief which was widely applied in rural England during the early nineteenth century. The only extensive series of crude birth-rate statistics available for rural counties are those compiled by Miss Deane and Professor Cole based on the aggregate totals of baptisms given in the Parish Register Abstracts. There is no indication in these of any significant increase in the fertility of rural populations during the late eighteenth and early nineteenth centuries. On the whole crude birth-rates in agricultural counties remained remarkably stable between 1750 and 1830. However, in view of the growing inadequacy of parish register baptism entries as guides to the total number of children born, little reliance can be placed on Deane and Cole's figures. It is possible that the relative stability of rural birth-rates simply reflects the increasingly serious problem of underregistration in the registers of the Established Church. Until we have a better guide to the evolution of rural fertility rates we must not overlook the possibility that the early population 'take-off' (before 1815 at least, when the demand for rural labour fell with agricultural depression) owed something to the effects of rising demand for labour on rural birth-rates.

A fresh look at the supposed demographic effects of the Speenhamland system has recently been taken by J. D. Marshall (*The Old Poor Law, 1795–1834*) and J. P. Huzel (*Economic History Review*, XXIII, 1969). Although far from being the final word on the subject, both studies reinforce the doubts which have long existed about Professor Krause's contention that poor relief operated as a powerful stimulus to the rate of population growth through its contribution to earlier marriage, and higher marriage and fertility rates. Huzel's work is of particular interest. In Kent during the 1820s and early 1830s child allowances were only provided for the fourth and subsequent children—a level of generosity which was hardly likely to cause a sharp rise in marital fertility. Not surprisingly, therefore, crude marriage- and birth-rates were no higher in parishes where the Speenhamland system was practised and where rates of relief were relatively generous (like Lenham) than in neighbouring parishes (like Barham) where Speenhamland was never adopted. On the other hand, Huzel's study does at first sight appear to offer some support to the argument first voiced by Dr Blaug—that Speenhamland relief contributed to population 'take-off' through its contribution to falling level of infant mortality. Infant death-rates (that is, deaths per thousand live births in the age-group 0–1) were certainly lower at Lenham than in the nearby parish of Barham, and they did fall slightly in the period 1821–35 when the Speenhamland system was in operation. Unfortunately, the Huzel-Blaug thesis is not strengthened by the fact that the modest decline in infant mortality rates at Lenham between 1821 and 1835 did not prevent a slight rise in crude death-rates, and cannot therefore have contributed to an increase in the pace of population growth. At Lenham anyway, the maintenance of high rates of population increase during the decade after 1821 owed nothing to the effects of the Speenhamland system on either fertility or mortality.

Of course the findings of one geographically limited study cannot be accepted as a complete refutation of the Krause and Blaug arguments, especially since it does not relate to the period between 1800 and 1820 when in most areas rates of poor relief were at their most generous. But what can be safely assumed at the present time is that the evidence we do have works against the notion that Speenhamland acted as a 'bounty on population'. A clear connection between the Speenhamland system and the early English 'population revolution' still remains to be demonstrated. And even if future research does show that a correlation existed between areas where Speenhamland relief was practised and areas where fertility was unusually high or mortality unusually low we will still be left with a problem. Was the adoption of a relatively liberal system of poor relief a cause or a consequence of variations in the levels of fertility or mortality? Could it be that the 'generous' allowances paid to the poor in Speenhamland areas were the result, and not the cause, of high birth-rates or low death-rates?

2. The Medical Case

Until the middle of the 1950s it was fashionable to believe that the 'population revolution' originated, at least in part, from a decline in mortality brought about by improvements in medical knowledge and practice. As long ago as 1825 the distinguished political economist J. R. McCulloch was writing

> The diminution of mortality has been going on gradually since 1750; and has doubtless been owing partly to the greater prevalence of cleanliness and sobriety among the poor, and the improvements that have been made in their diet, dress and houses, partly to the drainage of bogs and marshes, *and partly, and since 1800 chiefly, perhaps, to the discoveries in medical science, and the extirpation of the smallpox* [my italics] (J. R. McCulloch, *The Principles of Political Economy*, Edinburgh, 1825).

A hundred years later, Talbot Griffith wrote

> In addition to these causes of [population] increase which were connected with the industrial aspect of the country, *another lay in the medical improvements of the time* [my italics]. The period saw the rapid development of the hospital movement, and the beginning and remarkable growth of the dispensaries. Medical education and scientific investigation were improved. Sanitary science and right principles in the treatment of such scourges as fever which thrived under insanitary conditions were advanced, though not necessarily for strictly scientific reasons. For our purpose, however, the important thing is the reduction in mortality which resulted whatever the scientific principles involved may have been. The practice of midwifery was greatly improved: certain diseases which in former times had been serious sources of mortality were reduced or abolished, and smallpox was greatly lessened after the middle of the period by the

introduction of vaccination (G. Talbot Griffith, *Population Problems in the Age of Malthus*, Cambridge, 1926).

Since then numerous scholars have placed some stress on the part played by one or other of a series of medical innovations—the increasing number of general hospitals and dispensaries, the introduction of institutional confinement and of more hygienic methods of midwifery for children delivered at home, the widening range of drugs, a growing recognition of the need to segregate infectious disease cases, the adoption of inoculation and later vaccination against smallpox, and so on.

This long-established view came under severe attack with the publication of two articles written by medical historians, the first by McKeown and Brown in 1955 (*Population Studies*, IX), and the second by McKeown and Record in 1962 (*Population Studies*, XVI). Whilst admitting that the more frequent use of mercury in the treatment of syphilis cases, of iron for anaemia sufferers, of cinchona for malaria victims, and of inoculation and vaccination against smallpox worked towards a reduction in death-rates, Professor McKeown and his colleagues argued that, taken together, the various medical innovations had little real effect on the general level of mortality. Those which clearly helped to save life were countered by others (the voluntary, provincial hospitals for instance) which actually increased death-rates. If mortality declined in the late eighteenth and early nineteenth centuries—and McKeown and Brown believe that it did—then the explanation must lie elsewhere.

The McKeown and Brown thesis quickly became the new orthodoxy, and it is still widely supported today. There are ominous signs, however, that it too is beginning to fray at the edges. On the one hand Dr Razzell has suggested that the introduction of inoculation against smallpox in the late eighteenth century had a much greater effect on rates of mortality and population growth than McKeown and Brown believed:

inoculation against smallpox . . . could theoretically explain the whole of the increase in population (during the late eighteenth century), and until other explanations are convincingly documented it must stand out as the best available (P. Razzell, *Economic History Review*, XVIII, 1965).

On the other hand Dr Sigsworth has questioned McKeown and Brown's outright condemnation of the new provincial hospitals, and, in the light of his work on the records of the York County Hospital, has suggested that the effects of hospitals on death-rates should be re-examined.

> . . . eighteenth-century hospitals may not have deserved the miserable reputation which they have acquired . . . (E. Sigsworth, *The College of General Practitioners, Yorkshire Faculty Journal*, June, 1966).

There is no doubt that the practice of inoculation (reinforced and later replaced by vaccination during the early nineteenth century) *contributed* to the 'take-off' in rates of English population growth after 1780. In those areas and among those social classes where mass inoculations are known to have occurred the number of deaths due to smallpox decreased sharply. Provided that the incidence of other fatal diseases and illnesses did not increase, the general level of mortality accordingly fell, and the pace of population growth accelerated. But can inoculation, as Razzell seems to imply, explain the *whole* of the population 'take-off'? Can it be regarded as the sole reason for the upturn in rates of demographic increase during the twenty years or so following 1780? To answer these questions affirmatively we must be able to prove two things: firstly, that smallpox was *the* most important cause of death in the pre-inoculation period, and consequently the principal means by which the rate of population growth was kept down; and secondly, that the practice of inoculation (and later, of vaccination) was sufficiently widespread in the eighteenth and early nineteenth centuries to result in a major reduction in mortality from the disease.

If inoculation and a successful attack on smallpox is to be regarded as the *sole* explanation for early English population 'take-off', deaths from smallpox in the pre-inoculation period need to have accounted for about one-third of all deaths. Most of the surviving contemporary data, however, reveal a very much lower ratio of smallpox deaths to total deaths than this. In England during the first half of the eighteenth century, for example, contemporary records suggest that smallpox accounted for only about 15% of deaths from all causes. In Sweden between

1751 and 1800 (where the figures may be more accurate) only 16%
of all those dying below the age of one year and 8% of all deaths
above the age of one were attributed to smallpox (M. Drake,
Population and Society in Norway, 1735–1865, Cambridge University
Press, 1969). Dr Razzell believes that these contemporary figures
grossly understate the true level of smallpox mortality: firstly,
because some deaths due to smallpox, particularly to fulminating
smallpox, went unrecognised; secondly, because most of the extant
contemporary statistics relate to urban populations and not to
those of rural areas where smallpox outbreaks were rarer but far
more deadly when they struck. Unfortunately, it is at these points
that Razzell's thesis is weakest. Certainly some deaths escaped
recognition. But how many? The short answer is that we simply
do not know, and Dr Razzell's study does little to help us.
Moreover, such evidence as does exist suggests that smallpox
outbreaks among rural populations were no more serious than
those which occurred in urban communities. In the small Bedfordshire parish of Eaton Socon during the widespread outbreak of
1712–14 only sixteen of the one hundred smallpox victims died.
During the epidemic of 1722 in the rural market town of Bedfordshire only 18.4% of all cases proved fatal. At Godmanchester
(Huntingdonshire), the reputedly serious epidemic of 1729 caused
only two deaths out of two hundred sufferers, and both of these
committed suicide. The onus still lies with Dr Razzell to provide
conclusive proof that smallpox fatalities were as drastically under-
reported as he claims, and that smallpox really did account for
one-third of all deaths in the pre-inoculation period.

Arguably, Dr Razzell also exaggerates the extent to which
inoculation was practised in England during the late eighteenth
century. Although there is abundant evidence to show that it was
increasing in popularity from the 1780s, it is also true that many
people remained hostile or at best undecided about it. There were
two reasons for this public hostility or uncertainty. In the first
place, inoculation was quite expensive. Inoculations which were
paid for by the parish overseers of Wilhamstead and Houghton
Conquest (Bedfordshire) in 1778 cost four shillings per head. At
Wilhamstead in 1787 Richard Dilly was charging five shillings
each. By the early nineteenth century the cost may have fallen.
At Cople (Bedfordshire) in 1802 seventy-four people were treated
at 2s 6d each, and at about the same time Mr Gaye, a physician

in the Bedfordshire parish of Shefford, was prepared to 'vaccinate' people at two shillings a time. Nevertheless, despite the fall in cost, the treatment of a whole family remained an expensive business among low-income rural populations. In the second place, ill-founded though it was, there existed a widespread belief that inoculation increased rather than decreased the risks of infection. An agreement signed in 1766 by the leading inhabitants of Dunstable threatening strong action against Thomas Warren if he should establish an inoculation clinic at his home typifies the common apprehension.

> *The danger of infection caused by inoculation* [my italics] must not only put a stop to the trade of this town in general, so long as the distemper continues, but the infection must endanger the lives of such inhabitants who have not had the same distemper, a great many not having had the same, and more especially as it must spread among the poor of this town, a great and heavy charge must be brought upon the said Parish (Bedfordshire County Record Office, Dunstable, P/72/27/1).

Admittedly this example is for a rather early date. Probably such fears lessened in the course of the late eighteenth and early nineteenth centuries. But they did not disappear altogether. In a letter dated 25th March, 1804, Joseph Pawsey, an agent for the Countess de Grey, wrote

> In consequence of smallpox at Clophill, *and inoculation for it and the cowpox* [my italics], they have brought smallpox into this village, and in the centre of it next door to Woods shop, at the house of James Elmor, his daughter about 18 and another daughter ill; fear we shall have to inoculate whole parish (Bedfordshire County Record Office, L30/11/215).

Vaccination too, when it was introduced in the early nineteenth century, met a good deal of opposition. In part this came from inoculators who were anxious to protect the established technique; some because the spread of vaccination threatened their livelihood, others because they genuinely believed that vaccination was less effective. In part it came from the very same fears which had delayed the general adoption of inoculation—that it was costly, that it spread smallpox to other persons, that it caused venereal disease, that it was an interference with the natural laws of God. Whatever the explanation, the supporters of Jenner's new technique claimed, probably rightly, that it was far less widespread in England than in other Western European countries where governments took positive steps to encourage its adoption. In London, for example, the National Vaccine Establishment managed to vaccinate a mere three thousand people each year in the period between 1808 and 1812, at a time when the annual number of births averaged forty thousand. Not until the 1840s did free vaccination become widely available in England and not until 1853 was vaccination made compulsory. Not surprisingly, serious smallpox epidemics continued to occur. In view of the undoubted hostility towards inoculation and vaccination in the half century or so following 1780, it is possible, therefore, that Dr Razzell has exaggerated the pace at which these practices were adopted. At present, there is no conclusive proof that the proportion of the population inoculated against smallpox was as high as Razzell claims.

If, as seems likely, Dr Razzell has overstated the relative severity of smallpox mortality in the pre-inoculation period and also the extent to which inoculation was practised during the late eighteenth century, we can only conclude that inoculation (and later, vaccination) contributed to, but did not *wholly* cause, the 'take-off' in rates of English population growth after 1780. Even then, some of the decline in smallpox mortality which occurred during the period may have simply been due to a natural reduction in the virulence of the disease, and not to the effects of inoculation and vaccination at all.

The results of recent work by Sigsworth, Cherry (*Population Studies*, XXVI, 1972) and Woodward (J. Woodward, *The Development of the Voluntary Hospital System to 1875* . . ., unpublished Ph.D. thesis, York, 1970) on the role of the new provincial hospitals in the eighteenth century stand in sharp contrast to McKeown and Brown's thesis that the voluntary hospitals increased rather than decreased rates of mortality. At both York and Norwich in-patient and possibly out-patient mortality was low (at Norwich, for instance, only 4–5% of the hospital's in-patients died); very few patients died as a direct result of surgery; risks of cross-infection within the hospitals were rare, in part at least because infectious cases were deliberately excluded; and a remarkably high percentage of patients were discharged as 'cured' or 'relieved' (at Norwich about two-thirds of all in-patients). To judge from Woodward's broader analysis the cheer-ful stories of York and Norwich were repeated elsewhere. Hospital standards were surprisingly high in the eighteenth and early nineteenth centuries, but at some stage towards the middle of the nineteenth century began to deteriorate under the twin pressures of a vast increase in the demand for treatment (the result of population growth and a rising number of 'industrial' accidents) and of inadequate financial resources to deal with it. It seems that McKeown and Brown were quite wrong to assume that because hospital conditions were so bad in the late nineteenth century they must therefore have been much worse in earlier periods. On the contrary, the percentage of in-patients cured and relieved fell after the middle of the century, while the percentage dying within the hospitals rose (though never drastically). We might therefore conclude that the new voluntary hospitals, of which there were about fifty around 1800, did contribute to some saving of life among the populations they served, and did facilitate the 'take-off' in English population from the 1780s. We cannot at the moment accurately quantify this contribution. But it was probably small. The ratio of in- and out- patients in the Norfolk and Norwich hospitals to the population of Norwich city between 1786 and 1871 was never better than 1:22, and in the late eighteenth and early nineteenth centuries varied between 1:30 and 1:45. Furthermore, the general hospitals usually refused to admit people suffering from infectious diseases (the principal cause of death in early nineteenth-century England), and children under the age of six or seven years (the age-group in which mortality-rates were greatest). Even so, the voluntary hospitals may nevertheless have made a partial contribution to falling death-rates. As Cherry concludes:

> . . . it [the Norfolk and Norwich hospital] successfully cured outright large numbers of patients . . . who otherwise would have died, while tackling effectively those cases whose ill-nesses were not a threat to other patients. . . . Second, by removing many of the sick poor from an inadequate

domestic environment and treating them quickly and effectively, the hospital helped not only the individual patient, but in the case of the family breadwinner, his dependants also. Given that a considerable proportion of the Norwich population was at the subsistence level . . . having low resistance to disease and living in insanitary conditions, then the illness of the breadwinner would soon threaten the whole family. Consequently, to reduce the duration of illness . . . would lead to far greater benefits to the health of the city population than might at first sight be apparent (S. Cherry, *Population Studies*, XXVI, 1972).

*   *   *

Summarising our argument so far it would appear that the 'take-off' in rates of English population growth between 1780 and 1850 was primarily the result of the following factors: the existence of an age-structure which had developed out of the 'bulge-generation' created around the middle of the eighteenth century, and which was particularly suited to relatively high marriage- and birth-rates and low death-rates; the vast increase in the demand for adult and child labour which encouraged earlier marriage and higher rates of marital fertility by raising the average level of *money* (though not *real*) incomes; the adoption of inoculation and vaccination against smallpox which reduced the number of smallpox deaths and contributed to a decline in general rates of mortality; and finally, the spread of the provincial hospital movement and of the use of drugs like mercury, iron and cinchona in medical treatment which also contributed to population increase through the contribution they made to falling mortality. On this evidence, therefore, the early English 'population revolution' was a response to both rising fertility and falling mortality.

The other oft-quoted explanations for the 'take-off' in the pace of English population growth between 1780 and 1850 do not stand up to close scrutiny. Before the middle of the nineteenth century high rates of demographic increase were not due to any positive rise in the level of real wages or in the standards of public health, personal hygiene and nutrition. The Industrial, Agricultural and Transport Revolutions of the late eighteenth and early nineteenth centuries had not yet proved of much benefit to the great mass of England's labouring population. Neither is there any real support for the view that the Speenhamland system of poor relief contributed to the increase in rates of population growth in those areas where it was widely applied.

* * *

Up to this point we have followed the practice adopted by most writers on English population history and have treated England's demographic experience between 1780 and 1850 in isolation, without referring to what was happening elsewhere in Western Europe. There is, however, one serious weakness in this approach. As noted in an earlier chapter, the 'population revolution' of the late eighteenth and early nineteenth centuries was not unique to England and Wales. It was common, to a greater or lesser degree, to many European countries, embracing societies which were at very different stages of economic, social and political development. By treating the English case in isolation from similar events elsewhere we are in some danger of placing too much emphasis on purely localised explanations to the possible neglect of more pervasive, general ones. If, for instance, we assume, as many writers do, that industrialisation, through its effect on the demand for labour, was the main agent of early English population 'take-off', how we are to explain the simultaneous increase in rates of population growth in backward agrarian societies like Ireland or in other parts of Europe where industrial development on any meaningful scale had yet to begin? It is, of course, perfectly possible that the causes of the initial 'population revolution' varied from area to area. No doubt to a certain extent they did. But in view of the crude similarity in the pattern of population trends in the various parts of Western Europe during the eighteenth and early nineteenth centuries it is surely wiser to assume that some common influence, or set of influences, was at work. As Miss Buer wrote a long time ago, 'the growth of population was European and therefore many of the causes of that growth were also European'. The difficulty lies in identifying this common influence. There are several possibilities.

Professor Habakkuk (*Population Growth and Economic Development since 1750*) has suggested that the one feature shared by most Western European countries in the late eighteenth and early

nineteenth centuries was a marked increase in the overall pace
of economic growth. The precise form which this took varied
from one society to another. In England economic growth was
characterised by the rapid development of all three main branches
of the economy—agriculture, industry and commerce; in Brabant
by agricultural improvement and the expansion of foreign trade;
in France and parts of Scandinavia by the introduction of a wider
variety of food crops, rising levels of agricultural output and
better methods of distributing food supplies from areas of surplus
to areas of scarcity; in Ireland by a change in the balance of the
economy from pasture to arable farming to meet the demands of
the English market for grain. But exactly how did economic
expansion bring about the increase in rates of population growth?
Clearly, not by leading to any immediate improvement in the
average standards of life. There is no real evidence to support the
view that living standards were rising consistently throughout
Western Europe during the late eighteenth and early nineteenth
centuries. As we have seen, even in England where the pace of
economic growth was most rapid, there is no sign that the average
levels of real wages, nutrition and environmental conditions were
improving before the middle of the nineteenth century. On the
contrary, for a time anyway, they may actually have deteriorated
for large sections of the population. Could it be then, as Professor
Habakkuk seems to suggest, that population 'took-off' because
economic development, whatever form it took, necessitated a
sharp increase in the size of the labour-force, thereby encouraging
people to marry earlier and have larger families even though there
was no concomitant improvement in the real standards of popular
welfare? We have argued above that industrialisation had precisely
this effect in England. But can the same explanation be used to
account for the dramatic upturn in rates of population growth
elsewhere in Western Europe? If Habakkuk's thesis is correct we
would expect to find evidence of a substantial increase in the
average levels of European marriage- and birth-rates during the
period. Unfortunately, it is at this point that his thesis parts
company with at least some of the known facts.

The debate still rages over whether the early 'population
revolution' in England and Ireland was due to rising fertility or
falling mortality. In the Scandinavian countries of Norway and
Denmark, however, where population data are relatively reliable,

there is no doubt that the demographic 'take-off' was the result of falling death-rates. In France too the primary mechanism at work seems to be declining mortality rather than rising fertility. For this reason alone it is difficult to accept Professor Habakkuk's contention. The stimulus to fertility brought about by increasing employment opportunities may have been a significant determinant of population 'take-off' in some areas, as in England for example. But it cannot be regarded as the common denominator which shaped the demographic experience of all Western European societies in the late eighteenth and early nineteenth centuries. We must look elsewhere for our 'European explanation', and particularly perhaps at those developments which might have led to a reduction in the general level of mortality.

Without doubt Western Europe as a whole in the period 1780–1850 was a far healthier place than it had been in the previous hundred years. Outbreaks of severe epidemic disease were notably less regular than they had been earlier in the century. In the absence of any positive indication that this was the result of rising standards of diet or public health could it have been due to the widespread adoption of certain improvements in medical practice? The two likeliest and best documented possibilities are, firstly, the spread of better hospital facilities and, secondly, the introduction of inoculation and vaccination against smallpox. As was the case in England, population 'take-off' in many Western European countries no doubt owed something to these innovations. But they cannot be considered as the sole, or even the principal, reasons for the increase in rates of population growth. There were few hospitals catering for the populations of the remoter, rural parts of Europe where rates of population growth were nevertheless also rising rapidly. It is true that inoculation and vaccination were widely introduced throughout Western Europe during the period but in at least two areas, England and Scandinavia, they cannot have played more than a marginal role in early demographic 'take-off'. In Norway, for example, inoculation did not spread much outside the western parts of the country, and even as late as the 1840s a significant proportion of the population had still not been vaccinated (M. Drake, *Population and Society in Norway, 1735–1865*, Cambridge University Press, 1969, pp. 49–54).

One final possibility remains—that the increase in rates of population growth in the various countries of Western Europe during the late eighteenth and early nineteenth centuries may after all have been simply the result of a quite fortuitous natural reduction in the severity of epidemic disease; that for some reason (or reasons) totally unconnected with human activity either the strength of epidemic virus diminished or the resistance of the human host towards such virus increased. Until recently no one had argued this view very forcibly. McKeown and Brown (*Population Studies*, IX, 1955), Helleiner (*Canadian Journal of Economics and Political Science*, XXIII, 1957), and Chambers (*The Vale of Trent, 1670–1800*) were among those earlier writers who hinted that the general 'take-off' in rates of population increase owed something at least to 'those changes in virulence and resistance upon which human effort had no influence'. But the clearest and most unequivocal statement of this case has had to await Professor Chambers' last publication (*Population, Economy and Society in Pre-industrial England*). As Professor Chambers writes:

> I think it is arguable that random biological causes operating in successive onslaughts on an already high death-rate were so powerful through to the middle of the eighteenth century that they could initiate long waves of demographic depression *independently* [my italics] of available per capita resources; and that conversely the absence of such biological factors could result in lowering the death-rate and in inducing a population rise to the point at which, on occasions, direct Malthusian checks might operate, as for instance in the boom of population in the century before the Black Death. In other words, it can be argued that the long-term trend in population change was non-economic in origin (J. D. Chambers, *Population, Economy and Society in Pre-industrial England*, Oxford University Press, 1972).

In his discussion of the factors responsible for the secular decline in English mortality rates which began in the second half of the eighteenth century, Professor Chambers acknowledges, and rightly so, the contribution made by the new provincial hospital system, by the use of quinine for the treatment of malaria (ague?) and by the growing practice of inoculation against smallpox. But he also takes pains to remind us 'of the degree to which the decline in the impact of disease was due to the changing nature of disease itself and of the part played by the factor of immunity, both on the part of those at risk and also on the part of the agents by which it was conveyed to its human victims'. Thus, the disappearance of bubonic plague from England in the seventeenth century was attributable mainly to the new immunity of the rat population to the plague bacillus or to a change in the nature of the flea species which carried the bacillus on the rat host. Similarly, the diminishing severity of the great eighteenth-century scourges, smallpox and to a lesser extent typhus, likewise owed much to an increase in natural immunity—this time among human populations who had been exposed to the diseases for so long that their bodies were becoming naturally more resistant towards them.

Why an exogenous amelioration in the virulence of epidemic disease or an improvement in human resistance should have occurred in the late eighteenth and early nineteenth centuries remains unclear. One possibility which has been tentatively canvassed for Sweden is that it may have originated from an improvement in climatic conditions (G. Utterstrom, 'Some population problems in pre-industrial Sweden', *Scandinavian Economic History Review*, II, 1954).

Although little work has been done on the relationship between population and climate, there does appear to have been a *crude* similarity in the pattern of population and climatic change over Western Europe as a whole since the Middle Ages. During the period of rapid population growth in the late eleventh, twelfth and early thirteenth centuries, Europe's climate was remarkably genial, with warm and dry summers, mild winters, and relatively few serious fluctuations in climatic conditions. During the long period of demographic stagnation and decline through the late thirteenth, fourteenth and into the fifteenth centuries, on the other hand, the European climate deteriorated sharply, with many more cool and wet summers, long and bitterly cold winters and great variations in conditions from one year to another. This is the period so vividly described as 'the golden age of bacteria'—a period in which the population of all European countries was decimated by frequent outbreaks of pandemic and epidemic disease. The temporary improvement in climate during the late fifteenth and sixteenth centuries was matched by a notable increase in rates of population growth. But then when climatic conditions once again deteriorated at some stage during the seventeenth century the pace of population growth also slumped, and remained low until the middle of the following century throughout the period known to climatologists as the 'Little Ice Age'. Finally, the 'take-off' in European population growth which began during the late eighteenth or early nineteenth centuries was paralleled by a gradual improvement in climatic standards, perhaps beginning from as early as the 1750s. By the middle of the nineteenth century Europe's climate was better than at any time since the early Middle Ages. Of course, the existence of a broad correlation between variations in climate and population does not prove conclusively that long-term trends in European population growth before 1850 were determined solely, or even primarily, by autonomous fluctuations in climatic conditions. Without knowing much more about the history of climatic change and about the ways in which climate exerted its influence on the levels of fertility and mortality, any such suggestion can only be regarded as premature. At the same time, however, until it has been demonstrated otherwise, we must continue to allow for the *possibility* that Western Europe became a healthier place in the half-century or so after 1780 simply because in some mysterious way the vagaries of climate (or of other natural determinants of disease incidence) lessened the frequency and intensity of epidemic disease outbreaks and/or raised the threshold of human resistance towards them. The absence of *positive* proof is no reason for rejecting the view that the general decline in Western European mortality rates between 1780 and 1850 (and hence the common upsurge in rates of population growth) was primarily the result of a natural, exogenous amelioration in the force of death-carrying viruses, for which human activity can take no responsibility. As Professor Henry has written in the context of French population history:

. . . we still do not know whether this reduction in disasters (in the late eighteenth century) was produced by man, the result for instance of economic progress, or whether it was just a piece of good luck, the continuation of which was made possible by the undeniable progress of a later period (L. Henry, 'The population of France in the eighteenth century', in D. V. Glass and D. E. C. Eversley (eds.), *Population in History*, London, 1965).

The idea that the 'revolution' in the pace of Western European population growth between 1780 and 1850 may have been due mainly to an autonomous 'natural' decline in the virulence of disease is not intended to imply that man, and the changes he wrought to his way of life, had no influence on the pattern of population growth during the period. Unquestionably, regional variations in rates of population increase around the general demographic trends owed a good deal to human actions. Thus in England, population 'took-off' earlier and increased more dramatically than in most other areas because of the additional stimulus exerted by industrialisation (working through higher fertility), inoculation and vaccination, the use of new drugs, and the spread of improved hospital facilities. In France, on the other hand, the relatively small upturn in rates of population growth in the late eighteenth and early nineteenth centuries was due to the deliberate limitation of marital fertility by large sections of the French population. But, if only because no one has yet satisfactorily proven that the early 'population revolution' was man-made, it is more and more tempting to believe that the common 'take-off' in rates of Western European population growth between 1780 and 1850 was the fortuitous consequence of a reduction in the virulence of epidemic disease or of a rise in human resistance towards it, both of which operated through the mechanism of falling mortality and for which man can take little responsibility. In which case, the factors responsible for the initial stages of population 'take-off' before 1850 were very different from those which permitted the continuation of high rates of population increase through the second half of the nineteenth and early twentieth centuries.

FURTHER READING

Books and Monographs

M. C. Buer, *Health, Wealth and Population in the Early Days of the Industrial Revolution*, London, 1926.

A. M. Carr-Saunders, *World Population*, Oxford, 1936.

J. D. Chambers, *The Vale of Trent, 1670–1800, Economic History Review*, Supplement 3, 1957.

J. D. Chambers, *Population, Economy and Society in Pre-industrial England*, Oxford University Press, 1972.

P. Deane and W. A. Cole, *British Economic Growth, 1688–1919*, 2nd ed., Cambridge, 1967.

M. W. Flinn, *British Population Growth 1700–1850*, London, 1970.

D. V. Glass and D. E. C. Eversley (eds.), *Population in History*, London, 1965.

G. T. Griffith, *Population Problems in the Age of Malthus*, Cambridge, 1926.

H. J. Habakkuk, *Population Growth and Economic Development since 1750*, Leicester, 1971.

J. D. Marshall, *The Old Poor Law 1795–1834*, Studies in Economic History, London, 1968.

S. Pollard and D. W. Crossley, *The Wealth of Britain 1085–1966*, London, 1968.

M. Reinhard and A. Armengaud, *Histoire Générale de la Population Mondiale*, Paris, 1961.

B. H. Slicher von Bath, *The Agrarian History of Western Europe, AD 500–1850*, London, 1963.

E. A. Wrigley, *Population and History*, London, 1969.

Articles

W. A. Armstrong, 'La population de l'Angleterre et du Pays de Galles, 1789–1815', *Annales de demographie historique*, 1965.

M. Blaug, 'The myth of the Old Poor Law and the making of the New', *Journal of Economic History*, XXIII, 1963.

E. J. Buckatsczh, 'The constancy of local populations and migration in England before 1800', *Population Studies*, V, 1951.

J. D. Chambers, 'Population change in a provincial town, Nottingham 1700–1800', in L. S. Pressnall (ed.), *Studies in the Industrial Revolution*, London, 1960.

S. Cherry, 'The role of a provincial hospital: the Norfolk and Norwich hospital, 1771–1880', *Population Studies*, 26, 2, 1972.

D. E. C. Eversley, 'A survey of population in an area of Worcestershire', *Population Studies*, X, 1957.

C. W. J. Granger and C. M. Elliott, 'A fresh look at wheat prices and markets in the eighteenth century', *Economic History Review*, 2nd ser., 2, 1967.

H. J. Habakkuk, 'The economic history of modern Britain', *Journal of Economic History*, XVIII, 1958.

H. J. Habakkuk, 'English population in the eighteenth century', *Economic History Review*, 2nd ser. VI, 2, 1953.

K. F. Helleiner, 'The vital revolution reconsidered', *Canadian Journal of Economics and Political Science*, XXIII, 1, 1957.

E. P. Hennock, 'Urban sanitary reform a generation before Chadwick', *Economic History Review*, 2nd ser., X, 1, 1957.

J. P. Huzel, 'Malthus, the poor law and population in early 19th-century England', *Economic History Review*, 2nd ser., XXII, 3, 1969.

R. E. Jones, 'Population and agrarian change in an eighteenth-century Shropshire parish', *Local Population Studies*, 1, 1968.

B. Keith-Lucas, 'Some influences affecting the development of sanitary legislation in England', *Economic History Review*, 2nd ser., VI, 3, 1954.

J. T. Krause, 'Changes in English fertility and mortality', *Economic History Review*, 2nd ser., XI, 1, 1958.

J. T. Krause, 'Some neglected factors in the English Industrial Revolution', *Journal of Economic History*, XIX, 1959.

J. T. Krause, 'Some implications of recent work in historical demography', *Comparative Studies in Society and History*, 1, no. 2, 1959.

J. T. Krause, 'Some aspects of population change 1690–1790', in E. L. Jones and G. E. Mingay (eds.), *Land, Labour and Population in the Industrial Revolution*, London, 1967.

W. L. Langer, 'Europe's initial population explosion', *American Historical Review*, LXIX 1, 1963.

P. Laslett and J. Harrison, 'Clayworth and Cogenhoe', in H. E. Bell and R. L. Ollard (eds.), *Historical Essays 1600–1750 Presented to David Ogg*, London, 1962.

T. McKeown, R. G. Brown and R. G. Record, 'An interpretation of the modern rise of population in Europe', *Population Studies*, XXVI, 3, 1972.

T. McKeown and R. G. Brown, 'Medical evidence related to English population change', *Population Studies*, IX, 1955.

T. McKeown and R. G. Record, 'Reasons for the decline in mortality in England and Wales during the nineteenth century', *Population Studies*, XVI, 1962.

P. Razzell, 'Population change in eighteenth-century England: a reinterpretation', *Economic History Review*, 2nd ser., XVIII, 2, 1965.

P. Razzell, 'Population change and economic change in eighteenth-
and early nineteenth-century England and Ireland', in E. L.
Jones and G. E. Mingay (eds.), *Land Labour and Population in
the Industrial Revolution*, London, 1967.

E. Sigsworth, 'A provincial hospital in the eighteenth and early
nineteenth centuries', *The College of General Practitioners, Yorkshire Faculty Journal*, June 1966.

E. A. Wrigley, 'Family limitation in pre-industrial England',
Economic History Review, 2nd ser., XIX, 1, 1966.

E. A. Wrigley, 'Mortality in pre-industrial England, the example
of Colyton, Devon, over three centuries', *Daedalus*, 97, no. 2,
1968.

4. *The 'Demographic Transition'*

The long period of rapid population growth which had lasted unbroken since the late eighteenth century came to an abrupt end in the second decade of the twentieth century. Annual rates of demographic increase, which had averaged between 1 and 1.5% in the years 1850–1911, slumped to a mere 0.5% between 1911 and 1920, rose marginally in the 1920s (0.6%), but fell back again in the 1930s (0.4%), and were then lower than at any time since the mid-eighteenth century. Throughout the inter-war period the level of English net reproduction rates remained consistently below unity.* In other words, at the existing levels of fertility and mortality (and assuming no proportionate increase in the balance of in- over out-migration), the absolute size of the population of England and Wales was at some stage in the future doomed to decline. Most contemporary writers were quite convinced that depopulation was imminent.†

Everything, therefore, seems set for the population beginning to decline in a few years' time—though the temporary

---

*The Net Reproduction Rate (which is usually based on the experience of females) measures the number of daughters who would be born to a group of girl-babies by the end of their child-bearing period, on the assumption that current age, specific fertility and mortality rates remain unchanged. A Net Reproduction Rate of above 1.0 (unity) means that the size of the population will continue to increase. A rate of less than 1.0, however, means that ultimately the absolute size of the population will fall.

†We now know, of course, that they were wrong. Rising rates of fertility since the Second World War have spared us the 'terrors' of depopulation—if only to raise the equally haunting spectre of overpopulation. (See D. V. Glass, 'Fertility trends in Europe since the Second World War', *Population Studies*, XXII, 1, 1968).

increase in the birth-rate will no doubt continue for a few more years as a result of the reunion of families after the war and of the provision of adequate housing accommodation. The real cause for alarm is not that some decades hence we shall almost certainly be a few millions less, but that if the same attitudes towards the size of family wanted continue, every generation will be smaller than the last, so that we shall be faced some time during the coming centuries either with a country nearly empty of people or (and this is perhaps more probable) with a people reinforced by immigration and consisting of a mixture of our present British stock with that of peoples mostly from Eastern Europe or Asia (E. M. Hubback, *The population of Britain*, London, 1947).

The root of the problem, as contemporaries clearly realised, was that although mortality had fallen steadily since the late nineteenth century, fertility had fallen even more rapidly. Between 1881–85 and 1936–38 crude death-rates for England and Wales as a whole fell by over seven points (from 19.4 to 12.0 per thousand total population); crude birth-rates, on the other hand, fell by over sixteen points during the same period (from 31.4 to 14.9 per thousand population). A rather more detailed indication of the extent of the fertility decline is given in the following table.

TABLE IV *The size of family by marriage cohorts, England and Wales, 1861–69 to 1940–44*

Marriages celebrated:

Marriages celebrated:		Marriages celebrated:	
1861–1869	6.16	1910–1914	2.82
1871	5.94	1915–1919	2.46
1876	5.62	1920–1924	2.31
1881	5.27	1925–1929	2.11
1886	4.81	1930–1934	2.07
1890–1899	4.13	1935–1939	2.04
1900–1909	3.30	1940–1944	2.08

Source: E. A. Wrigley, *Population and History*, London, 1969.

It is the main purpose of the present chapter to explain why this long-term decline in fertility occurred.

First of all though, what was the demographic mechanism(s)

by means of which the secular decline in birth-rates was brought about? In theory, there are several possibilities. Falling fertility could, for instance, have been the result of a continuous reduction in the level of human fecundity, that is, in the physiological ability of men to impregnate and/or of women to conceive. Or, it could have been due to a long-run decrease in rates of nuptiality —the average age at marriage might have risen, smaller proportions of the adult population might have got married. Or, finally, it may have been the result of a greater tendency among married couples to practise birth control. It is important that we decide at the outset which of these mechanisms was at work.

'We have very little evidence about reproductive capacity (fecundity) at present, and still less about its past history.' So concluded the authors of the Royal Commission on Population in 1949. Unfortunately, this conclusion still remains true today. We know, of course, that the level of human fecundity can vary between different population groups and, within the same population group, between different periods in time. We are also aware of some of the factors responsible for such variations—the mental and physical health of a population, its age-structure (since reproductive capacity varies inversely with age), the differing lengths of the lactation period after child-birth, and so on. What we do not yet know is how these various factors have combined to influence the evolution of human fecundity since the late nineteenth century. There is to date no exact quantitative measure of recent changes (if any) in man's reproductive capacity; indeed, in view of the difficulties involved in measuring the level of human fecundability there probably never will be. In the absence of precise data all that we can do is consider the balance of probabilities.

On the one hand we must group all those writers who have argued that the level of natural fecundity has declined over the last hundred years or so. Many of the explanations given in support of this view now appear to be quite ludicrous. How seriously, for example, are we meant to treat the suggestion that the long-term decline in French fertility was caused by psychological repercussions arising from the popular craze for cuddling dolls or poodles, or the suggestion that it was the result of unmentionable physiological disorders stemming from the modern vogue for bicycle-riding? Other explanations—those, for instance, which see the decline in fecundity as a consequence of the tendency of modern populations to wash more frequently, to eat too much, or to eat food which has been ruined by the application of chemical fertilisers—perhaps warrant more serious attention, but not much more, and there is no real evidence to support any of them. Perhaps the most convincing argument is that which attributes a decline in fecundity to the increasing demands made on human nervous energy by the greater intensity and competitiveness of life in the complex modern world. Conceivably, one way this might have worked was by leading to a decrease in the frequency of sexual activity. Herbert Spencer was one of many late nineteenth-century writers who believed that the hurly-burly of modern urban living diverted man's interest and energies away from reproductive activities. Walter Bagehot, though with rather more reservations than most, was another:

> There are a variety of 'laws', some that can be clearly indicated, others that can be only suspected, which diminish or seem to diminish the multiplying capacity of mankind.
>
> One of these is the increase of intellectual action. Physiologists say, on a priori grounds, that if you spend nervous force in one direction, you will not have as much to spend in another . . . Hardly anyone who observes can doubt that women of much mind and fine nerves, as a rule, seem not so likely to have children, or, at least, not to have so many children as others (W. Bagehot, *Economic Studies*, 7th ed., London, 1908).

According to this view the sexual fatigue induced by over-indulging one's mental faculties has a lot to answer for.

On the other hand we must group all those writers who argue that the process of economic and social modernisation has been accompanied by—and, indeed, has been largely responsible for—an increase in the level of natural fecundity. Better standards of diet and medical care together with the vast improvement in environmental conditions have, so the argument runs, so far raised the level of physical well-being that men and women marrying in the 1930s were physiologically much more capable of reproducing the species than were those of earlier generations. In concluding that fecundity had increased rather than decreased, the Royal Commission of 1949 placed particular emphasis on the significance of the reduction in the frequency of venereal disease, and in the incidence of rickets (which can cause pelvic deformities).

Summarising the balance of probabilities it is probably safe to conclude that *if* there has been any change in the level of human fecundity in England since the 1870s it has almost certainly been for the better. The potential stimulus to man's reproductive capacity which derived from improvements in his physical condition has outweighed the potential loss of fecundity arising from the greater stresses and strains associated with modern urban-industrial life. Accordingly, the long-term decline in fertility which occurred in England and other relatively advanced countries from the late nineteenth century cannot be accounted for by a continuous decline in the levels of human fecundity. After all, if a decrease in man's reproductive capacity really was responsible for the secular decline in birth-rates between the 1880s and the 1930s, how do we account for the long-term rise in rates of fertility in the period after the Second World War? Surely not by claiming that the mental tensions of everyday life became any less serious than they had previously been?

The broad outline of variations in the rate of nuptiality in England and Wales since 1871 is given in Table V.

In all three age-groups considered, the proportion of men and women ever married (i.e. married, widowed, or divorced) decreased steadily throughout the period 1871 to 1911. The decrease was especially noticeable in the two youngest age-groups, 20–34 years, which were affected by the trend towards a later average age at marriage. In part, then, the initial stage of the long-term fall in rates of fertility was simply the result of a decline in the rate of nuptiality, particularly among young adults. Similarly, the dramatic and prolonged upturn in fertility after the Second World War was also partly determined by changes in the levels of nuptiality—in this case by their substantial increase. But what of the period between the world wars? Long-run trends in marriage habits during the 1920s and 1930s are somewhat obscured by the nature of the data for 1921 and 1931. The rate of nuptiality was abnormally high in 1921 (except among women aged 45–54 years) because of the short-term effects of post-war demobilisation and the customary marriage boom which follows the culmination of hostilities; and it was unusually low in 1931

TABLE V *The proportion of the population ever married, by sex and age-group, England and Wales, 1871–1951.*

Date	Age-group					
	20–24		25–34		45–54	
	M	F	M	F	M	F
1871	23.3	34.8	68.4	71.1	90.3	87.9
1881	22.3	33.5	68.3	70.7	90.4	88.1
1891	19.5	29.9	65.7	67.4	90.0	87.6
1901	17.4	27.4	64.1	66.0	89.0	86.6
1911	14.3	24.3	61.4	64.5	87.8	84.2
1921	17.8	27.4	65.9	66.3	88.0	83.6
1931	13.9	25.8	64.8	67.0	89.2	83.6
1939	17.4	34.4	66.3	71.0	90.5	83.3
1951	23.8	48.2	72.8	81.8	90.8	84.9

Sources: B. R. Mitchell and P. Deane, *Abstract of British Historical Statistics*, Cambridge University Press, 1962.

J. Hajnal, 'Aspects of recent trends in marriage in England and Wales', *Population Studies*, I, 1, 1947.

because the English economy was then in its worst phase of depression. The truth is that the rise in nuptiality which was such a feature of the post-1945 world had begun as early as 1911 and, as the figures for 1939 indicate, was particularly evident in the second half of the 1930s. Yet, in spite of this reversal in the direction of nuptiality trends during the 1920s and 1930s, the level of fertility continued to proceed downwards. We are forced to conclude that the relationship between nuptiality and fertility was not always a direct, positive one. Although decreasing marriage rates must be accorded some of the responsibility for falling fertility in the several decades before the outbreak of the First World War, they were obviously not responsible for the continued decline in fertility during the several decades thereafter.

It might at this point be worth digressing briefly to consider why the rate of English nuptiality followed this pattern. Why was there such a pronounced movement away from the married state between 1871 and 1911? Why did nuptiality rates begin to rise again during the inter-war period? Surprisingly, very little work has been done on the economic (and social) determinants of recent *long-term* variations in the average age at marriage and the proportion of people marrying.* There is, however, no doubt that long-term variations in the popularity of marriage since the 1870s were at least partly determined by secular changes in the pace and character of economic growth. Many nineteenth-century writers, in their reaction to Malthus' gloomy prognosis, argued that an increasing tendency to postpone marriage was an inevitable outcome of economic development. The point was well made by the Reverend Richard Jones:

> The wants of mankind are divided into primary and secondary. Primary wants are a given quantity, and include whatever is necessary to subsistence and health. Secondary wants are an unlimited quantity, embracing whatever contributes to comfort and enjoyment. Now, when a man's rank and estimation in society depend upon his ability to gratify his secondary wants, there is a strong inducement to him to defer marriage. It may be laid down as a rule, therefore, that the number of secondary wants is the cause determining the influence of moral and prudential motives in restraining from marriage. (W. Whewell (ed.), *Literary remains, consisting of the lectures and tracts of the late Reverend Richard Jones*, London, 1859.)

In other words, as an economy develops so does the effective desire for 'secondary wants', and so too do the pressures in favour of postponing marriage.

For the nineteenth and early twentieth centuries anyway, before

---

*The relationship between *short-run* variations in economic conditions and marital status is not considered here. For a discussion of this see D. V. Glass, 'Marriage frequency and economic fluctuations in England and Wales, 1851–1934', in L. Hogben (ed.), *Political Arithmetic*, London, 1938. Significantly, the strength of the correlation between marriage rates and real wages has decreased in the twentieth century with the spread of birth control practices.

the widespread adoption of modern birth control techniques offered an alternative means of controlling fertility, there may be a good deal of truth in this contention. As Professor Banks (*Prosperity and Parenthood*) has shown, the English middle classes (and no doubt some skilled lower-class groups too), in their anxiety to grasp the economic and social rewards offered by an industrialising society, had already begun to adopt new and more prudential attitudes towards marriage as early as the 1830s. Their willingness to defer marriage intensified during the latter part of the nineteenth century under the threat which the so-called Great Depression seemed to pose to their future material and social prosperity. After the First World War, however, the situation changed. Firstly, shocking though conditions were for the unemployed millions, for those in regular work* average levels of real earnings rose steadily throughout the inter-war period, and this provided a sounder material basis upon which to support earlier marriage and higher marriage-rates. It is no coincidence that the greatest increase in levels of nuptiality during the 1920s and 1930s occurred after 1933 when the domestic economy began its recovery from the worst depths of depression. Secondly, and perhaps more significantly, the greater availability of effective methods of birth control now provided for many more people than ever before a viable alternative means of guarding against the economic disaster which a large family might cause. As birth control techniques gained in popularity the postponement of marriage ceased to be the only reliable means of limiting marital fertility. With contraception, a large family was no longer an unavoidable corollary of youthful marriage. For this reason too, rates of nuptiality were encouraged to rise.

In addition to the part played by changes in economic conditions and contraceptive habits, variations in the extent of nuptiality in any population also depend on its sex structure, more precisely on the ratio of men to women in the marriageable age-groups.

---

*People who would in any case rely less and less on the postponement of marriage to keep their fertility rates down because they would be the first to adopt the regular practice of birth control techniques within marriage.

TABLE VI *The number of females per thousand males by age-groups, England and Wales, 1871–1951.*

Date	Age-group					
	15–19	20–24	25–29	30–34	35–39	40–44
1871	1010	1106	1111	1090	1093	1084
1881	1008	1093	1087	1077	1069	1079
1891	1014	1122	1115	1073	1059	1075
1901	1019	1119	1126	1100	1074	1062
1911	1016	1113	1115	1091	1072	1077
1921	1027	1176	1209	1186	1156	1127
1931	1009	1056	1061	1132	1185	1167
1939	997	1009	1032	1036	1048	1177
1951	1025	1023	1017	1034	1036	1030

Sources: J. Hajnal, 'Aspects of recent trends in marriage in England and Wales', *Population Studies*, I, 1, 1947.

B. R. Mitchell and P. Deane, *Abstract of British Historical Statistics*, Cambridge University Press, 1962.

The most striking feature revealed by the data in Table VI is the fall which occurred after 1911 in the ratio of women to men in the marriageable age-groups.* Throughout the 1920s and 1930s the balance between the sexes gradually became more equal, especially in the younger adult age-groups (15–29)—the age-groups in which marriage is normally celebrated. Just as the low rate of nuptiality (and thus of fertility) in the years between 1871 and 1911 was in part the result of an unusually large excess of women over men, so the rise in nuptiality rates during the inter-war period was in part due to the emergence of a more balanced sex-ratio in the adult population.

In theory, variations in the sex structure of a population depend on two factors: changes in the *relative* rates of male and female mortality; and changes in the pattern of migration. In the English case the former has been of little significance. The more important influence has been that exerted by fluctuations in the net balance between in- and out- migration.

---

*The abnormally imbalanced sex-ratio of 1921 was a temporary aberration brought about by the relatively heavy loss of male life in the Great War.

The great bulk of scholarly literature dealing with the causes of the great migrations of people from Europe in the late nineteenth and early twentieth centuries does ample justice to the enormity of the movement. Most of it has been concerned with trying to identify and explain the various *short-term* fluctuations in the number of people emigrating overseas. The debate has raged furiously between those who see the ups and downs in the tempo of migration as a reflection of short-run variations in the attractiveness of overseas opportunities (i.e. the strength of the 'pull'), and those who see them as primarily the response to variations in conditions at home (i.e. the strength of the 'push'). Thus, according to the first interpretation, the main peaks of emigration correlate with periods of particularly attractive opportunities overseas; while, according to the second, they are linked to particularly unattractive conditions at home. In a sense the division between 'pull' and 'push' factors is an artificial one. Individual or family decisions to emigrate would invariably take into account conditions both at home and abroad; what mattered was the *relative difference* between domestic and overseas opportunities. In any case, the fact that relatively attractive conditions abroad were (after 1870 anyway) often paralleled by relatively unattractive conditions at home makes it extremely difficult to decide whether 'push' or 'pull' considerations weighed uppermost in people's minds. The English experience is a good example of the problems involved.

According to Professor Brinley Thomas (*Migration and Economic Growth*) up to the 1870s the main peaks of migration from Britain to the United States *preceded* the upturn in rates of American economic growth, suggesting that at this stage at least emigration was determined primarily by the influence of 'push' factors at home (the chief of which being variations in the rate of population growth and in the relative severity of population pressure on food resources). From 1870, however, the situation becomes rather more complicated. From then until the outbreak of the First World War the principal surges in migration from Britain to the United States appear to *follow* upturns in the pace of American economic activity. At first sight this seems to suggest that international migration was now primarily a response to the varying strength of the 'pull' factors overseas (principally to fluctuations in the level of New World demand for European labour). But—

and here is the difficulty—the rhythm of economic growth in the USA and other debtor countries generally varied inversely with that in Britain. When the American economy boomed the British economy stagnated, and vice-versa. Thus, when the 'pull' factors were at their strongest so too were 'push' factors, and it is therefore quite impossible to decide to which we should give primacy. At the micro-level the simultaneous operation of both 'push' and 'pull' elements has been demonstrated by Ross Duncan (*Economic History Review*, 16, 1963–64) in his study of assisted migration from Cornwall and Gloucestershire to New South Wales. The number of emigrants fluctuated directly with variations in the strength of the particular 'pull' factor involved—in this case the size of the financial allocation voted by the New South Wales government to assist with the costs of passage and settlement. But the main peaks of emigration from Cornwall and Gloucestershire also correlated closely with the periodic onset of severe economic depression at home. Here too, then, it is difficult to separate 'push' from 'pull' influences. Short-run variations in the extent of migration were clearly determined by the nature of conditions both at home and abroad.

It is less difficult to explain why the period from the mid-nineteenth to the early twentieth century *as a whole* was characterised by a vast increase in emigration from Europe. Simply put, the phenomenon of mass overseas migration was the inevitable consequence (as well as being itself a partial cause) of the emergence and rapid growth of a free-flowing multilateral international economy. It was a logical outcome of the fact that there were overseas economies, in North and South America particularly, which for the first time were in urgent need of, and capable of, absorbing large inputs of European labour; of the fact that, temporarily anyway, the opportunities for a decent standard of life were much greater in the New World than at home. And it was all made possible by the recent development of cheap and relatively swift means of international travel and communications, which not only spread the word about the 'golden' opportunities that existed overseas but also made it easier for Europe's ambitious or disenchanted millions to reach them. When, in the 1930s, the net balance of international migration swung back into Europe's favour it did so primarily because the *relative* attractions of the New World had decreased. On the one hand, the opportunities available overseas for would-be emigrants were restricted by the severity of the slump in primary-producing countries, by the sharp decline in overseas demand for unskilled labour, and to a lesser extent by the imposition in certain countries of quota restrictions on the number of immigrants. On the other hand, life in Europe became, or at least *seemed* to become, more attractive— with the further spread of industrialisation, the extension of state welfare schemes, the reduction of population pressure following upon the general decline in birth-rates, and the emergence of a new spirit of nationalism (which was actually reinforced in some countries by anti-emigration legislation). Life in Europe during the 1930s was certainly grim, but it can hardly have been very much better abroad.

Whatever its causes, the relevant point to note here is the effect that migration had on the sex composition of England's population. The fact is that six out of every ten emigrants were males, heavily concentrated in the young adult age-groups. Accordingly, the mass exodus of people overseas in the several decades prior to the First World War greatly increased the excess of females over males in the young adult population remaining at home.* This, in part, explains why rates of nuptiality, especially among women, were so low in the period between 1870 and 1911. When the drain of young men overseas slowed down in the 1920s and halted altogether in the 1930s, the level of nuptiality among young adults, and particularly among young women, began to rise again.

The continuous decline in the level of English fertility during the period with which we are concerned was therefore not caused by a steady decrease in natural fecundity, and was only in part the result of a rise in the rate of celibacy among young adults. Rather, it was due to an increase in the practice of birth control techniques by married couples. According to Judah Matras (*Population Studies*, XIX, 2, 1965), the estimated proportion of married women who made a deliberate effort to control their fertility rose from 19.5% in the cohort born between 1831 and

---

*In most societies, and nineteenth-century England was no exception, the number of females in any case exceeds the number of males. This is because mortality rates are invariably higher among males than females.

1845 (marrying in the period between the 1850s and the 1870s) to
72.1% in the cohort born between 1902 and 1906 (marrying
during the 1920s and 1930s). Again, of all informants to the 1959
Marriage Survey who had begun their family-building before
1930 some 53% had at one time or another resorted to birth
control practices. In the cohort marrying during the 1930s, however, the proportion had risen to 65.5% (Rowntree and Pierce,
Population Studies, XV, 1961–62). As the practice of family limitation techniques gained in popularity childbirth came to be
increasingly concentrated in the early years of married life, and
the average age of the mother at the birth of her last child fell
drastically. Thus, married women born in 1851 (marrying in the
1870s) had given birth to approximately half of the total number
of children they conceived by the time they were thirty years old.
Compare this with the generation of married women born in 1911
(marrying in the 1930s) who had given birth to almost two-
thirds of all the children they were to conceive by that age
(Carrier, *Population Studies*, IX, 1955).

The transition of English fertility rates from the relatively
high levels associated with the pre-industrial world to the much
lower levels found in modern, economically-advanced societies
was, then, achieved primarily through the mechanism of birth
control. But why in the course of economic and social modernisation does the practice of contraception become more common?
What particular features of life in the modern world 'persuade'
people to limit the number of children they conceive?

It will be as well to be quite clear at the outset what questions
we are setting ourselves to answer. Fundamentally, any discussion of the causes which underlay the recent secular decline in
English fertility must deal with two specific issues. Firstly, why,
in England as in all advanced societies, has economic and social
development been accompanied by the spread of family limitation
and the acceptance of lower fertility norms? Secondly, how do we
account for the fact that in England and elsewhere in Western
Europe the general decline in fertility began in the late nineteenth
century?* Let us take each of these questions in turn.

---

*As noted in Chapter II, this statement should not be taken to
imply that birth control techniques had never been practised
before the late nineteenth century. Variations in social class

'The explanation (for the deliberate limitation of births within marriage) lies, we think, in the profound changes that were taking place in the outlook and ways of living of the people.' So concluded the authors of the Royal Commission on Population in 1949. What kind of changes did they have in mind?

1. Mortality and the Status of the Child

Foremost among the 'profound changes' working in favour of family limitation was the notable secular decline in infant and child mortality rates which began during the second half of the nineteenth century. Variations in the level of infant and child crude death-rates in England and Wales since 1841 are given in Table VII and represented in Graphs IV and V below.

TABLE VII *Deaths per thousand by sex and age-group, England and Wales, 1841–1935.*

Year	Males			Females		
	0–4	5–9	10–14	0–4	5–9	10–14
1841	68.4	9.6	5.1	58.6	9.2	5.4
1851	72.9	8.7	4.9	63.0	8.6	5.3
1861	71.8	6.7	4.3	62.0	6.8	4.4

fertility, *possibly* due to the practice of birth control within marriage, long pre-dated the 1880s (Carlsson, *Population Studies*, XX, 2, 1966; Loschky and Krier, *Journal of Economic History*, XXIX, 3, 1969). In at least one British social class, the nobility, the long-term decline in fertility had already begun by the early nineteenth century (Hollingsworth, *The Demography of the British Peerage*). In certain European countries too the initial onset of the fertility transition seems to have begun much earlier than the late nineteenth century (W. D. Camp, *Marriage and the Family in France since the Revolution*, New York, 1961; M. Livi-Bacci, 'Fertility and population growth in Spain in the eighteenth and nineteenth centuries', *Daedalus*, Spring, 1968; M. Livi-Bacci, 'Fertility and nuptiality changes in Spain from the late eighteenth to the early twentieth century', Part I, *Population Studies*, XXII, I, 1968). Even so, in England and most other advanced countries of Western Europe, a continuous decline in the level of *national* fertility rates only became significant from the 1880s.

Year	Males			Females		
	0–4	5–9	10–14	0–4	5–9	10–14
1871	71.7	8.3	4.4	62.4	7.5	4.5
1881	56.6	5.8	3.2	48.0	5.7	3.2
1891	64.6	4.7	2.6	53.7	4.7	2.9
1901	59.0	4.0	2.3	49.5	4.1	2.4
1911	46.7	3.5	2.1	39.5	3.4	2.1
1921	32.3	2.8	1.8	25.8	2.7	1.8
1931	22.4	2.3	1.5	17.4	2.0	1.5
1935	17.9	2.1	1.4	14.2	1.9	1.3

Source: B. R. Mitchell and P. Deane, *Abstract of British Historical Statistics*, Cambridge University Press, 1962.

In the age-groups between five and fourteen years the mortality rates of both boys and girls began to fall more or less continuously from the late 1860s or early 1870s onwards. In the youngest age-group, 0–4 years, the onset of the secular decline in death-rates was somewhat delayed, getting under way only around the beginning of the twentieth century. But once begun it proceeded very rapidly. Thus, in the period between 1901 and 1935 the mortality rate of children below five years of age fell by 67% for boys and 71% for girls.

The great saving of life which began during the second half of the nineteenth century followed mainly from a reduction in the incidence and fatality of infectious diseases like tuberculosis, typhus, typhoid, scarlet fever and smallpox. Professor McKeown and his colleagues have explained why this happened. (McKeown and Record, *Population Studies*, XVI, 1962; McKeown, Brown and Record, *Population Studies*, XXVI, 3, 1972). Basically, falling mortality was a result of two factors: slowly rising standards of popular diet from the 1850s; and improving conditions of public health—better methods of water supply and waste disposal, from the 1880s, and, later, better housing. Except for the contribution of vaccination to the decline in smallpox mortality, the part played by advances in specific medical therapies was negligible, at least until the introduction of chemotherapy in the mid-1930s. But falling death-rates were also a result of an entirely new desire to ensure the health and welfare of the individual, and particularly the health and welfare of infants and young children. The motives underlying this greater concern for individual well-being were only partly humanitarian. They were just as much a consequence of the late nineteenth- and early twentieth-century quest for 'national efficiency'—a quest which was itself a response to the challenges posed by a rapidly changing world. At a time when national birth-rates were already beginning to fall and when so many young adults were being lost to migration overseas, the survival and well-being of those who were born and of those who remained at home became all the more important. Quite apart from humanitarian considerations, the need to ensure the welfare of the child made good sense both economically and politically.

For some years, both in the press and on the platform, I have been endeavouring to draw public attention to the degeneration which to my mind is taking place in the physique of our two populations . . .; but if . . . it be shown,

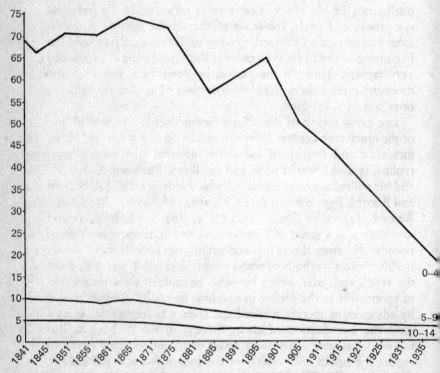

GRAPH V   *Deaths per thousand males by age-group, England and Wales, 1841–1935.*

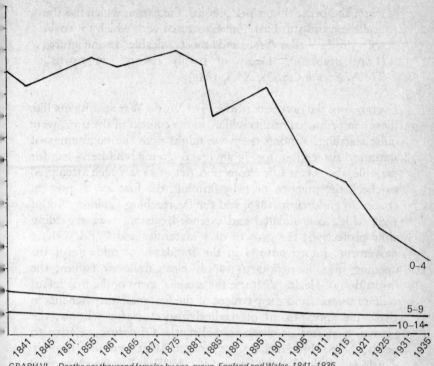

GRAPH VI   *Deaths per thousand females by age-group, England and Wales, 1841–1935.*

as I firmly believe it will, that large numbers of the inhabitants
of our cities are physically unfitted, though in the prime of
life, to defend the country in time of war, or to carry on her
work in time of peace, a growing but hidden danger to
Great Britain will have been revealed . . . the remedy which
naturally suggests itself is the minimizing of the unhealthy
conditions of urban life which have led to such a sad result—
in other words the better housing of the poor, the establishment of breathing spaces such as parks and playgrounds, the
feeding of the children in the National Schools, . . . the due
enforcement of sanitary laws, and finally the compulsory
training of all children attending Board and National
Schools in gymnastics and calisthenics. . . . The arts of peace
cannot be carried out successfully by men and women feeble
in body and weak in health. Physical strength is almost as
much required in the peaceful contests of everyday life as in

8

wars; and other things being equal, the nation which has the healthiest and sturdiest human material with which to work, will produce the best and most saleable manufactures (Lord Brabazon, 'Decay of bodily strength in towns', *The Nineteenth Century*, XXI, 1887).

Even before the outbreak of the First World War sentiments like these had produced results which, in the context of the time, were quite startling. Among them we might note the beginnings of statutory protection for infants and young children—as, for example, the Infant Life Protection Act of 1872 which attempted to check the practice of baby-farming, the first act to prevent cruelty to children in 1889, and the far-reaching Children Act of 1908 which consolidated and extended existing laws regarding child-protection; the growth of a Maternity and Child Welfare movement; improvements in the standards of midwifery; the opening of milk depots to supply clean milk for babies; the institution of Health Visitors; the establishment of the first infant welfare centres, and the payment of the first maternity benefits in 1911; the appointment of medical inspectors for schools; the provision of free or cheap school meals. Of course, relative to needs, these achievements were modest. Most were not properly developed until after the Second World War. But from the very start they made at least some contribution to the secular decline in infant and child mortality rates which was such a marked feature of the period with which we are concerned.

In the context of our discussion about the spread of birth-control the relevance of all this is simply that as mortality fell and as more children survived the perilous early years of life so the need to practise an effective form of contraception inevitably intensified. In pre-industrial times the one factor that had made high fertility possible, and indeed desirable, was that such a high proportion of those who were born did not live long enough to become a serious material burden on their parents. As infant and child death-rates declined, the potential drain on parental incomes increased, and it became quite impractical for parents to conceive as many children as they once had; hence the resort to lower fertility norms and the increasing adoption of birth control techniques to ensure them. But this was only one of many factors working towards a decline in birth-rates.

Another was the gradual emergence of a clearer realisation that high rates of fertility bred poverty. The Utilitarians and Neo-Malthusians* had, of course, long recognised this, and even before the middle of the century were urging contraception as the solution to working-class poverty. However, until the late nineteenth and early twentieth centuries their pleas invariably fell on deaf or uncomprehending ears. What was needed was a final and utterly unequivocal demonstration of the truth of their contention. This was to be provided by the findings of the massive statistical inquiries into social conditions, of which those by Booth and Rowntree are only the most famous. As Rowntree showed some 22% of the primary poverty in the town of York in 1889 was caused directly by the financial strains imposed by a large family. Firm statistical evidence of this kind helped to prove to all the inherent wisdom of the birth-controllers' arguments.

Coincidental with the decline in infant and child mortality rates and with the more widespread recognition of the fact that high fertility bred poverty went a continual rise in the net costs of raising children. Throughout the late eighteenth and early part of the nineteenth centuries the rapid and largely unregulated expansion of the English economy had offered unrivalled opportunities for the employment of young children, both inside and outside the home. Admittedly, child labour was not an entirely new phenomenon, but never before the early days of the Industrial Revolution had children been exploited on so vast a scale. For a time during the initial phase of industrial 'take-off' the income that children were able to earn in gainful employment led to a sharp reduction in the net costs of their upbringing; and, as we have argued in the previous chapter, this acted as a powerful stimulus to the levels of marital fertility. In the course of the second half of the nineteenth and early twentieth centuries, however, statutory legislation as embodied in the long series of Factory and Education Acts gradually restricted the range of

*Neo-Malthusians may be defined as those who accepted Malthus' fears about the danger of overpopulation while rejecting his proposed solution, moral restraint, as being unrealistic. Instead they advocated the practice of birth control within marriage—a solution which was unthinkable to Malthus himself.

opportunities available for child employment. Forster's Act of
1870 established the first national system of elementary education
for children between the ages of five and thirteen years inclusive,
and in 1880, with certain partial exemptions for children over ten,
school attendance was made compulsory. Then, in 1918, the
Fisher Education Act revoked all concessions for early leavers and
enforced full-time education for all up to the age of fourteen.
By the beginning of the inter-war period, therefore, young
children had at long last been completely removed from the
gainful labour force, and were no longer able to contribute
towards the costs of their upkeep.

Over the same period as legislative restrictions were being
placed on child employment, and thus on the opportunities for
child earnings, the level of parental expenditures on their children
was itself steadily rising. We will have more to say about the
reasons for this in the following section. It is enough to note here
that as economies modernise and technologies become more
sophisticated so the need for a well-trained, well-educated population grows. An advanced modern economy cannot be run effectively by people who have attained positions of influence and
responsibility through methods of selection based on the exercise
of patronage and family connections alone. Nor can it function
properly unless its labouring populations have been adequately
trained to carry out the relatively high-order skills demanded of
them. Furthermore, in the course of economic modernisation, as
the emphasis on education and training intensifies, the basic
determinants of social status themselves change. Social position
comes to depend much less on the mere accident of birth, and
much more on acquired talent and the suitability of one's talent
to meet the ever-changing requirements of a complex technological age. To a greater extent, and for a much larger section of
society, than ever before social promotion (and social demotion)
becomes a real possibility. The popular response to all this is
easily predictable; to prepare their children to meet the challenges
and opportunities which economic development affords, parents
are forced to spend a much higher proportion of their income
on their children's upbringing. Thus, in the late nineteenth and
early twentieth centuries, the English upper classes began their
cry for public school education; the rapidly-growing white-collar
urban middle-classes worked and saved to provide their offspring

with a decent education in the new secondary schools; the more progressive, 'better-off' sections of England's labouring population intensified their interest in the technical education provided by mechanics institutes, technical schools and colleges. How far this parental willingness to spend more on their children penetrated the lower echelons of English society is difficult to judge; probably, for most of the period with which we are concerned, not very far. Among the labouring population perhaps the most important factor militating against the maintenance of high fertility norms was not so much an increase in the level of parental expenditures on their children but rather the restrictions placed by the State on child labour, and hence on the opportunities for children to supplement the family income. In any event, whatever the explanation, the fact remains that all groups in society from the mid-nineteenth century onwards were confronted with the problem of increasingly expensive children, and were therefore provided with an additional incentive for limiting the number they conceived.

Conceivably, among lower income groups anyway, one of the most pressing reasons for bearing large numbers of children in pre-modern times was the security which children afforded to their parents in old age. In the absence of a state-controlled welfare system to cope with the material and social problems of the elderly, the potential comfort offered by a large family must have been a powerful, if subconscious, stimulus to fertility. The situation changed with economic modernisation. In the first place, the development of an urban-industrial economy has had a considerable effect on the nature of family life. The increase in social and geographic mobility that economic development gives rise to has greatly weakened the strength of family ties. The family in twentieth-century England is no longer the closely-knit economic and social unit that it once was. As a result, it has become less and less capable of catering for the needs of the elderly. This might have had particularly serious consequences because in some respects the problems of old age actually increase in the course of economic modernisation. The great pace of life in the modern world is a source of major difficulty to many old people. So too is the complexity and anonymity of the urban environments in which they live. Fortunately, with the help of countless voluntary societies, the State has stepped in to fill the breach. Over an increasingly wider and wider area, responsibility for the aged, once largely the function of the family, and when necessary of the local community, has been taken over by the State and placed on a centralised national basis. All this has had a significant, depressing effect on levels of marital fertility. Given the inability of the modern family to act as a protector of the elderly, and given also the willingness of the State to guarantee basic minimum standards for old people yet another rationale for large families has gradually disappeared.

2. *Materialism and the Process of 'Social Capillarity'*

As the authors of the Royal Commission on Population noted in 1949:

> The industrial and agricultural revolutions carried with them a shift from settled, traditional ways of life, in which changes came slowly, to new ways of life in which changes were liable to be frequent and abrupt. The old settled ways of life, in which ties of family and community were strong and in which most persons accepted the station into which they had been born, were passing. They were being succeeded by an intense competitive struggle in which the emphasis was increasingly placed on the individual rather than the community. Opportunities for 'getting on' were multiplied, but, at the same time, it became increasingly necessary to struggle to keep one's job and one's place in the community. . . . In general, it can be said that as the nineteenth century advanced more and more people were being thrown into the struggle for security and social promotion. There seems no reason to doubt that this process, which Arsene Dumont called 'social capillarity', helped the spread of family limitation in Great Britain. In the individualistic competitive struggle, children became increasingly a handicap, and it paid to travel light. The number of children tended to be limited also, not merely because the expenditure upon them might handicap parents in maintaining their own standards or achieving their ambitions, but because the fewer the children in the family the more could be spent on each child, and the better start it might have in life (Royal Commission on Population, *Report*, London, 1949).

There is no doubt that they were right. Two particular features of advanced industrial societies are worth remembering in this context. Firstly, as an economy develops, the range of cheap consumer goods broadens and the average level of consumer real incomes rises. For the first time, the bulk of the population, even of its lower income groups, is presented with a real possibility of aspiring to wholly new and hitherto quite unimaginable standards of comfort—provided, and this is an important proviso, they manage their spending wisely. Secondly, as we have previously mentioned, in the course of economic modernisation the degree of social mobility increases. In part this occurs because complex industrial economies demand a much wider variety of skills and occupations than did their predominantly agrarian predecessors. Industrialisation spawns new occupations, which in turn breed new social classes and additional rungs on the social ladder. As the gap between one social class and another narrows, the possibility of social promotion becomes more realistic. Individual ambitions for social advancement therefore increase, and so too does the likelihood that these ambitions will be attained. In part also the increase in social mobility which accompanies economic development stems from the fact that economic modernisation alters the criteria upon which social status is based. In pre-industrial times social status was determined primarily by birth and the workings of patronage and family connections. With the coming of the industrial age, however, the status accorded to an individual in society has come to depend much more on the nature of his education and training, and is determined primarily by the value which society places on his acquired expertise. The point to note about this transition is that a social hierarchy based primarily on talent is certain to be a good deal more fluid than one based largely on birth. Talent, after all, can be acquired. Moreover, the particular type of expertise needed by advanced industrial economies is constantly changing. In the march of technological progress today's urgently-needed skills often quickly become obsolescent. The story of the handloom weavers and later on of the coalminers, both once the very pinnacle of the 'labour aristocracy', are perfect illustrations of this. The continual demand for new skills and new aptitudes offers a constant stream of fresh opportunities for social advance. New elites continually emerge to challenge the structure of the established social order. And, as they do so, the status of the existing social elites becomes increasingly more difficult to maintain. In the modern world the threat of slipping down the social ladder is every bit as great as the possibility of climbing further up it.

The inevitable outcome of a rise in standards of life and of an increase in social mobility is the emergence of a much keener interest in the whole question of social status and of a much greater concern to ensure ever-higher material and social standards for oneself or one's children. However, at the income levels which prevailed among the bulk of the population in England during the late nineteenth and early twentieth centuries the task of translating the desire for social promotion into actual achievement was not an easy one. The costs of preparing a child to succeed in the race for social prestige were high. For all but the very wealthiest families (who could afford both) a choice had to be made between economic and social advance on the one hand, and high fertility on the other. For the overwhelming majority of people it was quite impossible to have both (as, indeed, it still is). Perhaps it was inevitable that the choice should fall on the former. As Professor Titmuss concluded, 'the acquisitive way of life must in the end mean that material things will take precedence over children'. (R. and K. Titmuss, *Parents' Revolt*, London, 1942). This was undoubtedly what happened in England and Wales in the decades after 1880, and it is probably the basic explanation of the long-term fall in rates of marital fertility.

3. *The Status of Women*

Yet another powerful ingredient in the reaction against excessive child-bearing was the gradual improvement in the status of the woman which accompanied economic and social modernisation.

The main stages in the process of 'female emancipation' in England are clearly indicated in parliamentary legislation from the late nineteenth century onwards. John Stuart Mill was no doubt right when in 1869 he wrote of the legal relationship between men and women that 'whatever is hers is his, but the parallel inference is never drawn that whatever is his is hers' (J. S. Mill, 'On the subjection of women', 1869, quoted by Ryder and Silver, *Modern English Society*). The married woman of the mid-nineteenth century had few rights and, in legal terms, scarcely any separate identity of her own. Slowly, too slowly for many, this changed. A succession of Property Acts, beginning in 1870 and culminating in 1893, gave married women the right to possess property of their own. In matters of divorce too their position gradually improved. Various acts passed between 1878 and 1902 allowed magistrates to grant separation orders with maintenance to wives whose husbands had been convicted of 'aggravated assault'. Then, in 1923, women were at last able to obtain a divorce on the grounds of their husband's adultery, as husbands had always been able to do. Even more obvious landmarks in the trend towards equality between the sexes came in 1918, when women over thirty received the right to vote, and in 1928, when all women over twenty-one were enfranchised.

All these legislative innovations certainly helped to further the cause of 'female emancipation'. But generally speaking legislation was itself merely a response to changes which had already occurred in the status of women. In reality, the movement towards greater sexual equality was a logical and inevitable outcome of the process of economic and social development. As the economy expanded so did the range of employments that were available for women, particularly in the service industries. Although the proportion of all women gainfully employed changed very little between 1881 and 1951, this masks a sharp rise in the proportion of *married* women in gainful occupations (C. E. V. Leser, 'The supply of women for gainful work in Britain', *Population Studies*, IX, 1955). The growing tendency for married women to take up employment outside the home was, of course, made possible by the diffusion of birth control techniques and practices. At the same time, however, we must not forget that the spread of contraception was itself stimulated by the very fact that such employment opportunities existed in ever-greater abundance.

The Victorian Feminist movement, which itself did much to further the cause of womanhood, was likewise very much a product of the changing times. It reflected the growing concern for the welfare of the individual. It also reflected the problems which had arisen from the rising surplus of women over men in the adult population. The aims of the Victorian Feminists have been analysed for us by Professor Banks (J. A. and O. Banks, *Feminism and Family Planning in Victorian England*). Initially, their concern was solely with the plight of the single and divorced woman. From the 1890s, however, they turned their attention more and more to the problems of the wife and mother, and came increasingly to question the traditional assumption that the sole function of the married woman was to procreate. From this point onwards, the Feminist lobby added its voice to the call for sexual equality within marriage, and for the first time gave public support to the campaign for family planning and lower fertility.

But, in the short run, perhaps the single most important factor contributing to 'female emancipation' (and thus to the reaction against excessive child-bearing) was the dramatic change in the status of women that was directly brought about by the First World War. The willingness of women to take on arduous occupations left vacant by men at the height of the war, and their obvious success in doing so, worked wonders for female morale, and greatly increased the respect accorded to the female sex. As Professor Marwick has put it:

> Through earning on their own account, they gained economic independence; through working away from home . . ., they gained social independence; through their awareness that they were performing difficult but invaluable tasks, were living through experiences once open only to the most adventurous, they gained a new pride and a new self-consciousness. . . . Of great significance was the escape from ill-paid, life-diminishing drudgery as dressmakers and domestic servants or low grade industrial labour into work which gave both economic status and a confidence in the performance of tasks once the preserve of skilled men (A. Marwick, *Britain in the Century of Total War. War, Peace and Social Change, 1900–1967*, Penguin Books, 1968).

It is quite clear that married women used the new-found equality which stemmed from events such as these to further the cause of birth control in order to free themselves from the burden of excessive child-bearing. It is also quite clear that their husbands were now more willing to accord with their wishes.

4. *Science and Rationalism*

There is, lastly, one other general factor, closely bound up with what we have rather loosely called the 'process of economic and social modernisation', which has exercised a significant, depressive influence on levels of marital fertility. The authors of the Royal Commission on Population called it 'the growth of science and new attitudes'. By this they meant two things.

Firstly, and most obviously, the development of modern science and technology has provided society with a wide range of cheap yet reliable and aesthetically acceptable mechanical and chemical contraceptives. The discovery of the process of vulcanising rubber in the mid-1840s made possible the subsequent mass production of rubber condoms which were altogether safer and more pleasing than the sheaths which from time immemorial had been fashioned out of an endless variety of other materials. Advances in chemical knowledge, as for instance the recognition of quinine sulphate as a spermicide, prepared the way for soluble pessaries, contraceptive jellies and pastes, and, ultimately, contraceptive pills—all of them far more reliable than the age-old techniques of the sponge or the post-coital douch.

Important though the improvements in methods of birth control were to the further diffusion of contraceptive practices, we should not exaggerate their contribution. It is not without significance that there was a long delay between the discovery of better methods of moulding synthetic rubber in the 1840s and the mass production and distribution of rubber condoms in the closing years of the century. In part, the development of new contraceptive techniques was itself dependent on the prior emergence of a large-scale market for them. Moreover, until very recently, the method of birth control most commonly practised, particularly among the working class, was that of *coitus interruptus*. Nevertheless, despite these reservations, it remains true that the long-term decline in levels of marital fertility which began in the late nineteenth century would not have been possible without the widespread availability of new mechanical and chemical devices.

The process of economic growth has also been responsible for causing a remarkable transformation in human ideals and attitudes. Rising standards of education, the growing interest in science and the successful application of scientific principles to the problems of everyday life, above all the incalculable uplifting psychological effect which came from man's obvious achievements in reshaping the structure of his environment have together given rise to an entirely new spirit of rationalism and optimism. The more man learned about himself and about the workings of his natural environment, the more he came to realise that the inadequacies of his society could be corrected by the application of human ingenuity and the redirection of human effort; and the less he was prepared to condone ideas and practices which appeared to be outdated or which seemed to lack an immediate rational purpose. 'Life came to be looked on, not as something to be passively accepted as the gift of God, but as something which man could and should plan and help to shape' (E. M. Hubback, *The Population of Britain*, London, 1947).

The tenets of established religion were among the first bastions of the traditional order to come under attack, and included among them were the attitudes of the Church towards family limitation. Until the nineteenth century Christianity had taught that the sole purpose of sexual intercourse within marriage was procreation. The practice of birth control (other than by abstinence from intercourse) was held to be an unnatural act, an abomination against the natural laws of God. In the pre-modern world, where a large population was much more a political and economic necessity than it is now and where a single epidemic could wipe out generations of population growth, the emphasis of both Church and State on the need to 'be fruitful and multiply' was understandable and perhaps justified. But it became much less rational in the nineteenth century when society took fright at the thought of overpopulation and when men began to make the connection between high rates of fertility and poverty. Even so, ardent churchmen like the Reverend Malthus, who was just as worried about the menace of overpopulation and the problem of poverty as anyone else, still refused to condone—refused even to consider—the adoption of what they continued to regard as 'unnatural practices'. In their view the population dilemma was to be solved (if, indeed, it was possible to solve it) by the use of techniques which accorded with the laws of God, that is, by the postponement of marriage and abstinence from sexual intercourse within marriage. This remained the official position of the Anglican church even as late as the 1930s, though its hierarchy was now fairly evenly divided between those who favoured birth control and those against it.

The fact is, however, that by the late nineteenth century the teachings of the Established Church, including its views on the proper methods of family limitation, had very little real influence on the habits of large sections of the community. Many people had either retreated from religion altogether (into apathy or agnosticism) or had turned to Nonconformist doctrines which seemed to be more relevant to the new environment in which they lived. As early as 1822 Francis Place had pointed to the absurdity and inhumanity of the assumption that celibacy and abstinence could be relied upon as effective means of keeping birth-rates down. It was futile, he said, to expect the working man to forgo one of the few pleasures open to him. Any lasting solution to the problems of overpopulation and poverty could only come from the dissemination of more effective techniques of birth control within marriage (N. E. Himes, *Illustrations and proofs of the Principle of Population by Francis Place*, London, 1930). For much of the first half of the nineteenth century such opinions made little headway against the staunch opposition of the Church and the powerful influence which Church doctrines still exercised in many quarters. But ultimately, with the rise of secularism and the decline in the influence of established religion, the way was cleared for Place's realism to gain more widespread acceptance. Indeed, by the closing years of the century, those who held to the Nonconformist faith—perhaps because of their more liberal theology, their greater stress on the freedom of the individual conscience, or their strong representation among the lower middle classes where the economic rationale for limiting fertility was strongest—were publicly urging the adoption of birth control as an agent of material progress. Thus, in the same way as the rise of the rational, scientific mind removed early Victorian taboos against the frank and open discussion of sexual questions, so it also weakened the ability of established religion to retard the diffusion of modern contraceptive techniques.

If English experience is any guide, the effect of economic growth on long-term variations in the level of human fertility appears to vary according to the particular stage of economic development concerned. Thus, in what we might call Stage I (which in England occurred during the late eighteenth and early part of the nineteenth centuries), the initial growth of the industrial economy positively encouraged earlier marriage and higher rates of marital fertility; and it did so primarily because of the unparalleled and unrestricted opportunities it offered for child labour. Subsequently, however, the further growth of the economy leads to the emergence of a society the nature of which militates against the maintenance of high fertility norms. In this Stage II (which England and certain other relatively advanced countries of Western Europe entered in the late nineteenth century), declining rates of infant and child mortality, the willingness of the State to take responsibility for the care of the elderly, the introduction of improved methods of birth control, the rising status of women, and above all the 'new', intense desire to ensure material and social advancement all combined together to force birth-rates down.*

We must not, of course, presume too close a relationship between the extent and character of economic modernisation and the level of fertility. Unquestionably, as Dudley Kirk pointed out some time ago (L. Dudley Kirk, *Europe's Population in the Inter-war Years*), there has been a crude correlation between the two, at least in modern European experience. Thus, in the various countries of North-West and West Europe, where economic growth was already well advanced by the late nineteenth century, the onset of the long-term decline in rates of fertility long predated the outbreak of the First World War. After the war, as the pattern of economic development spread through Southern and Eastern Europe, so too did the transition of fertility from high to low levels.† There are, however, a number of exceptions which

---

*Theoretically, as living standards rise still further, it is *possible* that a Stage III will emerge—one in which per capita real incomes are sufficiently high to allow families to acquire all the consumer goods they desire and also to have larger numbers of children than they do at present. Indeed, among the wealthiest social groups in the most advanced societies this stage may already have been reached. Compare the above argument with D. M. Heer, *Demography*, 3, 2, 1966, and *Daedalus*, 1968, upon whose work it relies heavily.

†Precisely which particular aspect of the 'modernisation process' was primarily responsible for causing the decline in fertility (if indeed any one factor can be singled out) remains uncertain. Carlsson (*Population Studies*, XX, 2, 1966) emphasises the primary importance of the fall in infant and child mortality rates. But the question remains open to debate.

mar the simplicity of this general rule. How, for example, do we explain the fact that fertility rates in France, Spain and the United States had apparently already begun their long-term decline from as early as the late eighteenth or opening years of the nineteenth centuries? Certainly not by assuming that these countries had already reached a relatively advanced stage of economic development. Again, how do we account for the maintenance of unusually high rates of fertility in so highly an industrialised country as the Netherlands? Quite obviously, then, there are influences which on occasions override and modify the effect which economic development has on levels of fertility. Birth-rates in relatively backward economies may be rather lower than one would expect if, for example, the population of such economies had close cultural contacts with communities practising low fertility norms. On the other hand, birth-rates in more advanced economies may be rather higher than expected due perhaps to the stimulus given to fertility by friction between competing ethnic or religious groups. Nevertheless, when all the proper reservations have been duly noted, the fact remains that it is to the process of economic and social modernisation that we must look for our explanation(s) of the long-term decline in fertility.

It remains, finally, to consider why the secular decline in rates of English fertility began (or, at least, first became noticeable) in the 1880s. Apart from the obvious fact that the structure of English society now met some at least of the basic requirements that we have described above as being essential to the emergence of lower fertility norms, two events in particular helped to speed the diffusion of birth control practices during the last twenty years of the century—the trial in 1877 of Charles Bradlaugh and Annie Besant for reissuing Charles Knowlton's pamphlet on birth control, 'The Fruits of Philosophy'; and the traumatic effect of the so-called Great Depression of 1873–96 on the expectations of the middle classes.

Until 1877 the arguments for and against contraception never entered the forum of public debate. Accordingly, the bulk of the population remained ignorant or indifferent towards the birth control question, and was thus quite unable to appreciate its relevance to their own lives. The Bradlaugh-Besant trial altered all this (J. A. and O. Banks, *Population Studies*, VIII, I, 1954). For the first time the pros and cons of the birth-controllers' case entered the arena of public discussion through the media of the national and local press, and did so in terms that were easily understood by all. It mattered little that the jury declared the book 'calculated to deprave public morals', or that the majority of the press agreed with this verdict. It mattered little that the Established Church and the medical profession (J. Peel, *Population Studies*, XVIII, 1964–65) remained hostile to the general adoption of birth control. What really mattered was the publicity accorded by the trial to the birth control issue. If widespread ignorance of the methods and rationale of contraception had retarded the earlier dissemination of family limitation practices, it was much less likely to do so after 1877.

A more important catalyst to the diffusion of contraceptive practices, however, was the threat which the Great Depression seemed to pose to the present and future standards of life of England's middle classes (J. A. Banks, *Prosperity and Parenthood*). Over the last few years historians have come increasingly to doubt whether in any meaningful sense there really was a serious depression between 1873 and 1896 (S. B. Saul, *The Myth of the Great Depression, 1873–1896*, London, 1969). Fortunately, whether there was or not is of little consequence in the present context. What does matter, and what is not in dispute, is that contemporaries genuinely believed conditions to be depressed. The beginnings of industrialisation abroad, growing competition in world trade, falling prices and the squeeze on profit margins came as a shock to businessmen and investors who had become accustomed to the unchallenged prosperity of the early Victorian period, and led to a serious decline in their confidence of what the future held in store. Coming at a time when the English bourgeoisie was more interested than it had ever been before in the pursuit of material and social status, the apparently gloomy economic prospects of the 1880s and early 1890s were perfectly calculated to impel middle-class society towards family limitation. If middle-class incomes really were about to stabilise, as was feared, a continued rise in the standards of life could only be assured by cutting back on the number of children conceived. Had future economic prospects not appeared to be so blighted, who can doubt that the onset of the secular decline in fertility would have been rather longer delayed?

What happened in England and Wales was by no means unique.

Other Western European countries also experienced the beginnings of a long-run decline in levels of fertility during the late nineteenth century, and here also it is perfectly proper for us to stress the catalytic effect of both the Bradlaugh-Besant trial and the Great Depression. The publicity accorded to the trial of Charles Bradlaugh and Annie Besant spread far beyond England. Economic depression, to a greater or usually lesser extent, was also a feature shared by many European countries in the closing decades of the century. Germany and the United States suffered prolonged industrial depression in the 1870s, though not in the subsequent decade. The French economy stagnated throughout the period from 1881 to the mid-1890s. As Professor Saul concluded, 'undoubtedly the fall in prices and the impact this had upon agriculture in particular in many parts of the world contributed to the feeling of gloom. Undoubtedly too, this was a period of rapid change and disturbance' (S. B. Saul, *The Myth of the Great Depression, 1873–1896*, London, 1969). Growing anxiety about the future at a time of increasing tension both between individuals and between nations was a widespread feature of the late nineteenth century European world: certainly pervasive enough to have acted as a general incentive to the rapid spread of birth control practices and to the start of the secular decline in levels of marital fertility.

FURTHER READING

Books and Monographs

J. A. Banks, *Prosperity and Parenthood*, London 1954.

J. A. and O. Banks, *Feminism and Family Planning in Victorian England*, Liverpool, 1964.

J. M. Beshers, *Population Processes in Social Systems*, London, 1967.

W. A. Carrothers, *Emigration from the British Isles*, London, 1929.

P. Fryer, *The Birth-controllers*, London, 1965.

T. H. Hollingsworth, *The Demography of the British Peerage*, London, 1964.

J. W. Innes, *Class Fertility Trends in England and Wales, 1876–1934*, Princeton University Press, 1938.

L. Dudley Kirk, *Europe's Population in the Inter-war Years*, Princeton University Press, 1946.

F. Lorimer *et al.*, *Culture and Human Fertility*, Paris, 1954.

D. Marsh, *The Changing Social Structure of England and Wales, 1871–1951*, London, 1958.

Royal Commission on Population, *Report*, London, HMSO, 1949.

J. Ryder and M. Silver, *Modern English Society. History and Structure, 1950–1970*, London, 1970.

Brinley Thomas, *Migration and Economic Growth. A Study of Great Britain and the Atlantic Economy*, Cambridge University Press, 1954.

R. M. Titmuss, *Birth, Poverty and Wealth. A Study of Infant Mortality*, London, 1943.

R. and K. Titmuss, *Parents' Revolt*, London, 1942.

D. H. Wrong, *Population and Society*, New York, 1966.

Articles

J. A. and O. Banks, 'The Bradlaugh-Besant trial and the English newspapers', *Population Studies*, VIII, 1, 1954.

G. Carlsson, 'The decline of fertility: innovation or adjustment process', *Population Studies*, XX, 2, 1966.

F. Campbell, 'Birth-control and the Xian churches', *Population Studies*, XIV, 1960–61.

N. H. Carrier, 'An examination of generation fertility in England and Wales', *Population Studies*, IX, 1955.

R. V. Clements, 'Trade unions and emigration, 1840–80', *Population Studies*, IX, 1955.

J. W. B. Douglas, 'Social class differences in health and survival', *Population Studies*, V, 1, 1951.

R. Duncan, 'Case studies in emigration: Cornwall, Gloucestershire and New South Wales, 1877–86', *Economic History Review*, 16, 1963–64.

C. Erikson, 'The encouragement of emigration by British trade unions, 1850–1900', *Population Studies*, III, 1949.

J. Hajnal, 'Aspects of recent trends in marriage in England and Wales', *Population Studies*, I, 1, 1947.

J. Hajnal, 'Age at marriage and proportions marrying', *Population Studies*, VII, 2, 1953.

D. M. Heer, 'Economic development and fertility', *Demography*, 3, 2, 1966.

D. M. Heer, 'Economic development and the fertility transition', *Daedalus*, 1968.

W. P. D. Logan, 'Mortality in England and Wales from 1848–1947', *Population Studies*, IV, 2, 1950.

D. J. Loschky and D. F. Krier, 'Income and family size in three eighteenth-century Lancashire parishes: a reconstitution study', *Journal of Economic History*, XXIX, 3, 1969.

J. Matras, 'Social strategies of family formation. Data on British female cohorts born 1831–1906', *Population Studies*, XIX, 2, 1965.

T. McKeown and R. G. Record, 'Reasons for the decline in mortality in England and Wales during the nineteenth century', *Population Studies*, XVI, 2, 1962.

T. McKeown, R. G. Brown and R. G. Record, 'An interpretation of the modern rise of population in Europe', *Population Studies*, XXVI, 3, 1972.

F. H. Amphlett Micklewright, 'The rise and decline of English Neo-Malthusianism', *Population Studies*, XV, 1961–62.

J. Peel, 'The manufacture and retailing of contraceptives in England, *Population Studies*, XVII, 1963–64.

J. Peel, 'Contraception and the medical profession', *Population Studies*, XVIII, 1964–65.

S. Peller, 'Mortality past and future', *Population Studies*, I, 4, 1948.

G. Rowntree and R. M. Pierce, 'Birth-control in Britain', Part I, *Population Studies*, XV, 1961–62.

W. S. Shepperson, 'Industrial emigration in early Victorian Britain', *Journal of Economic History*, XIII, 1953.

G. J. Stolnitz, 'A century of international mortality trends', I, *Population Studies*, IX, 1955.

5. Population and the Economy

So far we have concentrated entirely on the *causes* of English population trends since the eighteenth century. But the relationship between demographic change on the one hand and economic and social development on the other is undeniably a two-way affair. Population movements are as much a cause as they are a consequence of variations in economic and social conditions. In this and the following chapter we must try to rectify the balance by looking at the way in which the population variable has influenced the course of economic and social development in England over the last two-and-a-half centuries. Let us begin by considering the economic consequences of recent demographic trends.

1. *Some Theoretical Considerations*

Theoretically, variations in the total size, the rate of growth and in what we might call the 'demographic composition' (i.e. nuptiality, fertility and mortality rates: age, sex and marital structures) of any social group affect the pace and pattern of economic progress in two ways: firstly, by helping to determine the size and efficiency of the labour force that is available for productive purposes; secondly, by helping to determine the extent and character of the effective market for goods and services of all kinds.

Of course, neither the quantity and quality of the labour force nor the level of aggregate demand are decided solely by demographic circumstances. The number of producers varies from time to time and between one society and another in part according to variations in the average ages at which individuals enter and leave the labour force, and these variations are a function of a wide range of economic, social and cultural factors. The quality of any work force is determined partly by the vast complex of circumstances which decide the physical and mental capacities of individual workers and the efficiency with which they are organised for production. Non-demographic conditions play an even more important part in determining the total size of the market. The old mercantilist dictum that the larger the population and the faster its rate of growth the larger and the more rapid would be the increase in demand for goods of all kinds has long since been proven false. Certainly, an increase in population will always lead to a rise in demand for those products which are essential to the maintenance of life (foodstuffs and the basic raw materials for clothing and accommodation), but it may not always result in a proportionate rise in the level of effective demand for other agricultural, industrial and commercial goods and services. If the size of a population, or the rate at which it grows, outruns its ability to provide foodstuffs and basic raw materials, aggregate demand for less essential products may well decline. Under such circumstances, as food and raw material prices rise, the proportion of total real incomes available for expenditure on less essential goods will fall, and as a result the pace of economic expansion will ultimately slow down. In short, a large and growing population will lead to an increase in the size of the market for secondary and tertiary products only if it does not encroach too far on the level of consumer real incomes and purchasing power. Whether or not it does so depends on man's ability to expand his stocks of foodstuffs and raw materials as rapidly as his total numbers are growing, and this in turn depends on a wide range of non-demographic as well as demographic factors. Up to a point population growth, and additional labour inputs, will itself generate a rise in the output of essential primary products. But after that point any further increase in per capita output depends on the introduction of new technologies and improved methods of production, the determinants of which are far more diffuse than the stimulus given by population growth alone. Finally, within the context of the theoretical relationship between population and demand, we must remember that in advanced industrial societies where average real incomes are comfortably above basic subsistence levels the size of the market for *particular* products is probably much more a function of variations in consumer taste than of changes in demographic structure. Among populations living closer to the margins of subsistence vagaries in consumer taste are somewhat less important determinants of the pattern of demand, but even here they cannot be ignored altogether.

Nevertheless, despite these reservations, the population variable does have a considerable influence on the pace of economic growth through its effects on both the number of producers and consumers.

As a general rule, the larger the population and the more rapid its rate of growth, the greater will be the absolute size and rate of expansion of its labour force. The 'fit' between the total size of a population and the total size of its labour force is not completely exact. Populations of the same size may have different numbers of producers and rather different productive capacities according to their respective age and sex structures. Thus (quite apart from differences caused by variations in the non-demographic determinants of productive capacity), very young or very old populations in which the ratio of people in the more active age-groups between fifteen and sixty-four years is relatively small, and populations with an abnormally large excess of females over males will have fewer producers and be somewhat less productive than those with better balanced age and sex compositions. Neither is there a perfect 'fit' between the rate at which populations grow and the rate at which their labour forces expand. In populations which are growing at a similar rate, the increments to the labour force may be relatively large or small according to the demographic mechanism by means of which the population has increased. Thus, variations in the rate of population growth that are based on alterations in the balance between in- and out-migration (usually a movement of young able-bodied adults, and particularly of males) will have a more immediate effect on the number of producers than will variations that are due to a rise in fertility or a fall in infant and child mortality (both of which would require a period of perhaps fifteen to twenty years to transmit their full effects to the labour force).

It is also generally true that in societies where the per capita supply of foodstuffs and essential raw materials rises, or at least remains stable, the larger the population and the more rapidly it grows the greater will be the size and rate of growth of aggregate effective demand for less essential goods. Once again, however, the relationship between the size and rate of growth of population on the one hand and the level of effective demand on the other is not absolutely precise. Apart from the effects of non-demographic characteristics like changes in consumer taste, variations in age and sex structures and in the number and composition of household and family units exert their own influence on the extent of the market for particular products. But as with the relationship between population and the number of producers, so the sheer size and rate of growth of a population remains a vital determinant of the number of consumers. In societies where real incomes are comfortably above basic subsistence levels and where the stocks of primary products can be expanded as quickly as population growth demands any further increase in population will act as a positive stimulant to the size of the market for the whole range of industrial and commercial goods and services. On the other hand, in communities where average incomes are dangerously near to subsistence levels and where foodstuffs and basic raw materials cannot be increased quickly enough to satisfy a growing population, any further growth in population may lead to a decline in aggregate demand for the goods of the secondary and tertiary sectors, and may thus retard the pace of economic development.

In theory, therefore, there is a close, working relationship between the size, rate of growth, age, sex, household and family composition of a population on the one hand, and its producing and consuming capacities on the other. What, briefly, are the consequences of alterations in the number of producers and consumers for the pace of economic expansion?

The economic effects of variations in the size of the labour force are by no means straightforward. In economies where there is a shortage of workers relative to needs the total output of, and investment in, productive enterprise will be restricted by high labour costs (since wages form a major part of production costs) and by the relative inflexibility of the labour supply. Under such circumstances an increase in the number of workers will curtail the rise of wages, create a more flexible labour force which can be more easily diverted from one form of production to another, and may therefore result in cheaper products, a higher level of entrepreneurial investment and activity, and an overall increase in both aggregate output and the general pace of economic growth. However, in economies where the supply of labour is already adequate for most needs any further increase in the number of workers may retard the future growth of the economy by discouraging labour- and capital-saving technological innovations, and perhaps also (through its effects in depressing the level of real wages) by reducing the level of effective consumer demand. In other words, the economic effects of variations in the supply of labour depend on how such variations affect the optimum relationship between the supply of, and demand for, workers.

A large and rapid increase in the size of the market for goods and services is obviously advantageous to an economy. Rising demand encourages greater specialisation and division of labour, an increase in the scale of production and, as a consequence, leads to a wider range of cheaper and better quality products (the availability of which generates a further growth in the size of the effective market). It also stimulates the level of entrepreneurial investment and activity since risk-taking innovations are much less dangerous when demand is growing rapidly, and when a business failure in one direction can be more easily remedied by investment in other, expanding, sectors.

*   *   *

Theoretically, therefore, the population variable has an important part to play in the process of economic development. In view of this it is surprising to note how little attention historians have paid to the *actual* role of demographic change in English economic experience over the last two hundred years or so. Whether because of the inadequacies of the available population statistics, or because of the daunting problems involved in trying to isolate and quantify the contribution of population to economic growth, the fact remains that very few scholars have ever looked closely at the practical economic consequences of England's recent demographic history. As a result what follows relies heavily on a small number of early pioneering efforts and undoubtedly leaves much still to be said.

2. *Population and Economic Growth, 1700–50*

By comparison with what was to follow in the second half of the eighteenth century, the period between 1700 and 1750 was one in which both population and total national product grew very slowly. According to the tentative calculations made by Miss Deane and Professor Cole (*British Economic Growth, 1688–1959*) the index of aggregate real output rose by a mere 25% in the first half of the eighteenth century, from base 100 in 1700 to 125 in 1750. In contrast, it more than doubled in the fifty years after 1750, reaching 251 by 1800. The coincidence of *relative* economic and demographic stagnation during the early part of the century was not purely fortuitous. Whatever else was to blame for the retardation in rates of economic growth, much of the responsibility must be shouldered by the simultaneous downturn in rates of population increase and its corollaries—the shortage and high cost of labour, and the slowness with which the aggregate level of demand for agricultural and industrial products grew.

Contemporary writers were in no doubt about the underlying causes of early eighteenth-century economic retardation. As Daniel Defoe observed in 1704:

> Having thus given an account of how we came to be a rich, flourishing and populous nation, I crave leave as concisely as I can to examine how we came to be poor again. . . . 1. I affirm that in England there is more labour than hands to perform it. This I prove 1st. From the dearnesse of wages, which in England outgoes all nations in the world (D. Defoe, *Giving Alms No Charity*, 1704).

As late as the mid-1750s, Josiah Tucker, in trying to discover why the population of England was so small, wrote:

> A country thinly peopled, has neither the Strength, nor Riches it would have, were it better inhabited. . . . The Lands must lie waste where there are no Markets: and the Artificers cannot be employed without Customers (J. Tucker, *The Elements of Commerce and the Theory of Taxes*, 1755).

To contemporaries, then, the root cause of England's economic malaise was a combination of high wages, insufficient supplies of labour and inadequate markets; and underlying all of these was the fact that 'England never was so populous as it might have been, and undenyably must now be far lesse populous than ever' (Anon, *Britannia Languens, or a Discourse of trade*, 1680).

In view of this diagnosis it is not surprising that the contemporary solution was a demographic one.

The odds in Populacy must also produce the like odds in Manufacture; plenty of people must also cause cheapnesse of wages: which will cause the cheapnesse of the Manufacture; in a scarcity of people wages must be dearer, which must cause the dearnesse of the Manufacture (Anon, *Britannia Languens*, 1680).

As the Numbers of People increase, the consumption of Provisions increase, more Lands are cultivated; waste Grounds are inclosed, Woods are grubb'd up, forests and common Lands are till'd, and improv'd; by this more farmers are brought together, more farm-houses and Cottages are built, and more Trades are called upon to supply the necessary demands of Husbandry. . . . As Trade prospers, Manufactures increase; as the Demand is greater or smaller, so also is the Quantity made. . . . Trade has increas'd the People, and People have increas'd Trade; for Multitudes of People, if they can be put in a condition to maintain themselves, must increase Trade; they must have Food, that employs Land; they must have Clothes, that employs the Manufacture; they must have Houses, that employs Handicrafts; they must have Household staff, that employs a long Variety of Trades (D. Defoe, *A Plan of the English Commerce*, 1728).

As that 'celebrated writer' Charles D'Avenant put it 'the bodies of men are . . . the most valuable treasure of a country; their encrease or decrease must be carefully observed by any government that designs to thrive' (C. D'Avenant, *Discourses on the Public Revenues and on the Trade of England*, 2 vols., 1698, Vol. II). In the short term some of the worst problems might be overcome by stiffening, or even abolishing, the poor laws in order to transform able-bodied idlers into active producers, 'to make the most of a labour force that was not keeping pace with demand' as Professor Chambers once remarked; or perhaps by encouraging immigration. But the ultimate solution could only come from a dramatic increase in the indigenous rate of population growth. This was the goal which the mercantilist propaganda effort sought to attain.

On the whole modern research supports the contemporary emphasis on the part played by demographic stagnation in the economic 'set-back' of the early eighteenth century. Of course, the relative failure of the English economy in the several decades preceding 1750 is now known to have been due to much more than demographic conditions alone. *Inter alia*, it reflected the bottlenecks caused by inadequate supplies of coal and iron; the reluctance of many landowners and merchants to commit themselves more fully to investment in the secondary and tertiary sectors of the economy; the 'persecution' of one of the most industrious groups in English society, the religious dissenters; the perpetuation of the Navigation Acts which in the short run anyway diverted capital away from industrial development and into colonial trade, shipbuilding and the wasteful military and naval expenditures essential for the success of the mercantilist programme; the absence of a financial and credit organisation sufficient to ensure the smooth flow of funds into industry. The list is by no means exhausted. But when full allowance is made for the other factors involved the basic explanation for the meagre performance of the English economy before 1750 remains the slow pace at which population grew.

In his classic study of the Vale of Trent, Professor Chambers has shown how the twin evils of labour shortage and limited markets combined to such an effect that the years from 1720 to 1750, when the rate of population growth was at its slowest, were ones 'of pause for capital; investment in enclosures, turnpikes and industrial enterprise has left little for the historian to record'. Inadequate supplies of labour meant higher wages, higher costs of production, and thus a general tightening in the level of demand for manufactured goods. They also help to explain why the character of the early industrial labour-force was so ill-suited to the discipline required by large-scale 'factory' methods of production. Lewis Paul was not alone among contemporary manufacturers in lamenting, 'I have not half my people come to work today, and I have no great fascination in the prospect I have to put myself in the power of such people.' The opportunities available for earning decent wages outside the factory or of making enough to live on by working for only part of the week were not likely to encourage regular attendance or conscientious work habits. Little wonder that the quality of, and hence the demand for, manufactured products was so poor.

Even more serious than the problems posed by labour shortage

were those arising from the very slow increase in the level of
aggregate demand. What happened has been described by Professor Chambers and by Miss Deane and Professor Cole. The
accidental association of an almost stationary population with a
series of abundant harvests led to a much slower growth than was
normal in the size of the market for food grains (though not, as
we shall see, for other agricultural products).

The result was that the real incomes of those sectors of the
agricultural community which lived by the sale of grain crops
also increased relatively slowly, if at all. Because such people
were still the single most important source of demand for industrial products and commercial services, and because also they
supplied much of the capital for investment in industry and commerce, the ensuing stagnation in their propensity to consume and
invest had a depressing effect on the performance of the economy
as a whole. Finally, it is worth noting that to the extent that
industrial profit margins were restricted by the limited growth
in the level of effective demand for industrial goods, manufacturers found it particularly difficult to introduce labour-saving
innovations which might otherwise have eased some of the worst
problems caused by inadequate supplies of labour.

* * *

How did all this affect the subsequent development of the English
economy? Did the long period of relative economic stagnation
in the first half of the century make later industrial 'take-off' that
much more difficult? At first glance it would appear that it did.
Although, in absolute terms, the industrial sector of the economy
did expand during the first half of the century (mainly in periods
of above average rates of population increase, in the opening
years of the century and during the late 1740s), manufacturing
industry was still in its infancy in 1750. The stock of industrial
entrepreneurs and factory-trained workers was small. The investing public still needed to be finally convinced of the merits and
profitability of investment in factory industry; and the amount of
capital so far accumulated in the industrial sector, which could
be 'ploughed-back' by businessmen of a future generation, was
not as great as might have been wished. Unquestionably, industrial
'take-off' in the late eighteenth century would have been much

smoother had the size of the industrial legacy been somewhat larger. For this weakness demographic stagnation in the period before 1750 must take a good deal of the responsibility.

One wonders, however, whether the absence of a broad industrial base in 1750 really mattered all that much in the long-term. It is, after all, arguable that the adverse legacy passed on by the stunted performance of the manufacturing sector during the first half of the century was outweighed by a more beneficial inheritance which derived from certain important 'structural' changes simultaneously taking place in the economy—'structural' changes which, incidentally, came about precisely because rates of population growth were so low. This point demands some elaboration.

The combination of demographic stagnation on the one hand and a substantial rise in the output of food grains on the other, particularly during the period between 1720 and 1750, had an immediate and unmistakable effect on the pattern of domestic consumer demand. As the real cost of basic food grains fell, the average level of real wages among those sections of the community which did not grow their own foodstuffs (perhaps by this time the majority of the population) rose. The result was that a large and rapidly growing proportion of the population was able to spend a greater percentage of its income on less essential foodstuffs like meat, dairy and market-garden produce, and, in addition, was for the first time able to enter the market for cheap manufactured products. None of this is in dispute. What is in dispute, however, are its economic consequences.

Some years ago Professor John (*Journal of Economic History*, XXV, 1965) argued that the market among low income consumers for cheap manufactured goods which had emerged in the period before 1750 largely disappeared thereafter, when the rate of population growth quickened and outran the supply of basic food grains. According to Professor John the golden age of working-class prosperity between 1720 and 1750 did not lay the first broad foundations of a permanent domestic mass market for the products of manufacturing industry. Higher rates of industrial growth in the second half of the century were primarily the result of an increase in overseas, not internal, demand. What happened before 1750 was of little lasting benefit to the future growth of the economy.

More recently, however, Professor John's thesis has been challenged by Dr Eversley ('The home market', in Jones and Mingay (eds.), *Land, Labour and Population in the Industrial Revolution*). According to Eversley, in spite of the pressures exerted by population growth and rising grain prices on the level of working-class real wages, the market for manufactured goods among low income consumers *did* survive into the second half of the century, and played a vital role in later industrial 'take-off'. Without it the sustained growth of the English economy may not have been possible. Dr Eversley supplies an impressive array of evidence to support this view, and his contention has been strongly supported by Professor Chambers (*Population, Economy and Society in Pre-industrial England*), though as Chambers implies the labouring population was not yet the *principal* source of demand for industrial goods (it did not become so until well into the nineteenth century). The crucial question is, of course, this: why were low income consumers able to continue their purchases of manufactured products after 1750? We will discuss this question more fully in the following section. For the moment let us note that part of the answer lies in certain developments which occurred in the agricultural sector of the English economy in the several decades before 1750.

The association of low grain prices and relatively high popular real incomes, particularly between 1720 and 1750, had a marked and permanent effect on the character of English agriculture. The urgent need to cut costs of grain production combined with the new opportunities afforded to livestock and dairy farmers, and to market-gardeners, led to a substantial improvement in the overall quality of English farming. The period before 1750 was marked by a gradual increase in the average size, and thus in the efficiency, of farming units; by a steady improvement in the working relationships between landlords and their tenants; by the spread of mixed arable-pasture farming, aided by the cultivation of new fodder crops like turnips, sainfoin and clover. Of course, large sections of English agriculture remained backward, and were quite incapable of responding to the novel challenges and opportunities which demographic stagnation had helped to bring about. In many parts of the country the pace of improvement was retarded by inherent conservatism, insufficient capital for investment, the small size of farms, the rigidities of the open-field system, and on heavy, clay soils by a failure to solve the basic problems of drainage. But innovation was the order of the day in the lighter soil areas of southern and eastern England, and in areas bordering on rapidly-expanding urban markets. This was enough to generate a sharp upturn in the levels of agricultural output and productivity, and in the standards of English farming as a whole.

The benefits of all this were not fully felt until the second half of the century when rates of population growth accelerated. Because of the earlier increase in agricultural efficiency, the supply of foodstuffs after 1750 was, contrary to Professor John's opinion, more or less able to keep pace with the rise in aggregate demand. The increase in food prices was therefore minimised, and the strain on working-class real incomes greatly reduced. As a result, the size of the domestic mass market for manufactured products in the latter part of the eighteenth century remained very much more buoyant than it would otherwise have been, and the process of industrialisation benefited accordingly. In passing it is worth noting also that the ability of English agriculture to meet the growing demands placed upon it after 1750 lessened the need for any drastic increase in food imports and, in so doing, prevented an excessive drain of capital overseas at precisely the time when it was required to finance the rapid expansion of the industrial and commercial sectors of the economy.

There remains to be considered one last long-term benefit, which emerged from the period before 1750 when rates of population growth were unusually low and consumer real incomes relatively high. Those of the labouring population who had enjoyed a higher standard of life in the several decades before 1750 were extremely reluctant to abandon their newly-acquired tastes after the mid-century when the level of money earnings stabilised, and for many perhaps even fell. The fact is that rather than sacrifice their new standards, labourers in both industry and agriculture were willing to work harder and longer in order to maintain them. The effect of this on the quality of the labour force in the late eighteenth century is emphasised by Professor Chambers:

One aspect of the Industrial Revolution that is often over-looked is that the labour force was not only very much larger but that it was worked very much harder. Increased output was not due entirely to new technology but increasing effort by those working in the traditional industries played its part (J. D. Chambers, *Population, Economy and Society in Pre-industrial England*).

Whether, on balance, the effects of low rates of population growth in the period before 1750 were an advantage or disadvantage to the subsequent development of the economy remains far from clear. It is, however, tempting to believe that any problems which might have stemmed from the very slow pace at which the economy grew before 1750 were ultimately more than offset by the stimulus that early eighteenth-century demographic retardation gave to the gradual emergence of a large mass market for industrial products and of a better quality labour force to produce them.

3. *Population and Economic Growth, 1750–80*

In the thirty-year period immediately following the middle of the eighteenth century the average rate of both economic and demographic growth accelerated noticeably. The population data have been given elsewhere. On the level of economic activity Miss Deane and Professor Cole conclude that whereas the rate of growth of total output averaged less than 0.3% per annum in the period between 1700 and 1745 'there can be little doubt that there was a marked acceleration in the rate of growth after 1745; for twenty years it averaged about 1% per annum, and although the pace slackened in the next two decades (to between 0.6 and 0.8%) it seems to have maintained a level which was more than double that prevailing in the early part of the century' (*British Economic Growth*, 1688–1959). Without wishing in any way to understate the importance of the many other factors involved, there is no doubt that the modest but quite definite upturn in the pace of economic activity after 1750 was largely due to the simultaneous increase in rates of population growth.

Long ago Professor Chambers demonstrated how a growing population cleared the way for economic advance by easing the problems previously caused by labour shortage. 'To the innovators of the sixties and seventies the labour force which had been conspicuous by its scarcity and truculence in the forties was no longer an obstacle to change; it was both more plentiful and was becoming more amenable' (*The Vale of Trent, 1670–1800*). But for the availability of a larger and more flexible supply of labour in the second half of the eighteenth century the pace of economic progress would have been immeasurably slower.

But an even greater contribution to economic growth came from the part played by an expanding population in stimulating the level of effective demand for industrial products. However, although historians generally accept that a higher rate of population growth was the basic factor underlying the rise in demand for manufactured goods in the period between 1750 and 1780, they are not agreed on the manner in which this was brought about.

On the one hand Miss Deane and Professor Cole (*British Economic Growth, 1688–1959*) believe that higher rates of population growth led to an increase in demand for industrial products, and hence to greater rates of industrial growth, through their effects on the consuming and investing propensities of those sections of the agricultural community whose incomes depended chiefly on the sale of food grains and on the rents of the land they leased to others. Quickening rates of population growth after 1750 meant a rise in grain prices and, because of the growing competition for tenancies among a rapidly increasing rural population, a substantial rise in earnings from rent. As the real incomes of farmers and landlords rose so did their demand for manufactured goods; so too, incidentally, did their investment in industrial, commercial and indeed agricultural enterprise. Since the 'marginal propensity of farmers and landlords to consume manufactured products was higher than that of wage-earners and the non-agricultural sector as a whole' (an arguable view, but one which best fits the pattern of population and economic growth in the eighteenth century), such a situation was guaranteed to stimulate the further development of manufacturing industry.

Dr Eversley ('The home market', in Jones and Mingay (eds.), *Land, Labour and Population in the Industrial Revolution*), on the other hand, sets out an alternative view of the relationship between population growth and rising demand. According to his interpretation the rise in domestic demand for manufactured goods during the thirty-year period after 1750 came from two sources: firstly, from a steady increase in the number of what he

describes as 'middle-class' consumers; secondly, and rather more
contentiously, from a continued increase in the aggregate level
of 'working-class' demand.

Few would dispute Dr Eversley's contention that with the
expansion of industry and commerce the number of middle-
income consumers increased in the course of the eighteenth
century, from perhaps one to three million, and that their total
expenditure on the products of manufacturing, mining and build-
ing rose from something like £10m. at the beginning of the
century to £30m. at the end. It has been argued above that he is
also correct in believing that the size of the 'working-class' market
for secondary products likewise expanded during this period. Of
crucial significance to the continued growth of working-class
demand between 1750 and 1780 was the behaviour of food prices.
If the price of basic foodstuffs had risen too quickly the ability of
the labouring population to purchase manufactures might well
have decreased. Fortunately, the rise in grain prices in the three
decades following 1750 was kept to within moderate proportions.
Why? Partly, as we have seen, because of the legacy of agricultural improvement left over from the period of demographic
stagnation in the first half of the century. Partly also because the
transport innovations of the third quarter of the eighteenth
century helped to keep costs of distribution down. But in part
simply because the rate of population increase was itself very
modest. Whether through some mysterious ability to control its
own rate of increase or, more probably, by pure chance, the pace
of English population growth in the period 1750–80 roughly
approximated to the pace at which the supply of food grains
could be expanded. Because there was no great rise in the price of
food grains the labouring population continued to have a margin
of income for expenditure on manufactured products (though no
doubt somewhat less on average than during the 'golden age' of
the 1720s and 1730s), and this together with the upturn in rates
of population growth after 1750 was enough to generate an
increase in the aggregate level of 'working-class' demand for the
products of the secondary sector.

The views expressed by Miss Deane and Professor Cole, and
by Dr Eversley are not necessarily irreconcilable, at least for the
years between 1750 and 1780. Perhaps both contain an element of
the truth. With population growing more rapidly than it had done

in the first half of the century the real incomes of landlords and farmers (part of Eversley's expanding group of 'middle-class' consumers) rose, and so did their demand for industrial products. At the same time rates of population growth were not so rapid as to erode completely the ability of the wage-earning sections of English society to purchase the cheaper manufactured items. The result was the final consolidation of a large domestic market upon which industrial and commercial expansion could build after 1780.

4. *Population and Economic Growth, 1780–1939*

As we have seen in an earlier chapter, in the last twenty years of the eighteenth century and throughout the long period from 1800 to the outbreak of the First World War, rates of English population growth rose to new and sustained heights. Thereafter, in the years between the world wars, the pace of demographic expansion slowed down markedly. We have already considered the extent to which this pattern of demographic evolution was fashioned by the forces of economic change. We must now look at the other side of the coin, and consider the influence exerted by the population variable on the pace and character of economic development during this period.

*   *   *

Until fairly recently the economic consequences of modern English population trends were assumed to be quite straightforward. The general view was that the acceleration and maintenance of high rates of population growth from the late eighteenth to the early twentieth century was a leading cause of the substantial and well-documented economic achievements of the age, whereas the decrease in rates of population growth after the First World War were largely responsible for the severe problems which beset the economy in the 1920s and 1930s.

According to this interpretation one of the main props of England's economic success in the nineteenth century was the emergence of a multilateral international economy and of England's ability to dominate it. Both the expansion of international trade and English dominance over it owed much to the fact that the rate of population increase was high. Let us look first at the ways in which a rapidly growing population contributed to the build-up of a world economy.

Some time ago, in a now strangely neglected article, E. C. Snow (*Journal of the Royal Statistical Society*, XCVIII, 1935) wrote that 'the mainspring of the development (of international trade in the nineteenth century) was the increase in population'. The rapid growth of population in the industrialising countries of Europe triggered off a vast increase in their demand for the foodstuffs and raw materials which the countries of the New World—North and South America, Australia, New Zealand—were equipped to supply. The income earned by primary producing areas in meeting these needs meant that they in turn could increase their demand for the manufactured goods produced by England and other European nations. Moreover, the cheap food imports made possible by the stimulus given to primary producing economies by European population growth were largely responsible for a notable rise in the level of average real wages among lower-income consumers in England during the latter part of the nineteenth century—and rising real wages at a time of rapid population increase gave a powerful boost to the size of England's own domestic market for industrial products. Without abundant sources of food supply from the New World, agricultural prices would have risen as population grew, and aggregate demand for all but the most basic essentials of life would probably have fallen.

Apart from the contribution they made to rising demand, high rates of population growth fostered the development of an integrated world economy in yet another way—by contributing to the emergence of a better balance in the international division of labour. The great migrations of people from Europe to the New World in the late nineteenth and early twentieth centuries, made possible, if not positively essential, by sustained population increase at home, helped to overcome a number of potentially serious problems. Chief among these was the threat posed to the future development of primary producing economies by the shortage of indigenous supplies of labour. Immigration solved the worst of the problem. It provided the manpower to run the farms and the factories, and to construct the roads and railways necessary for transporting goods to and from the ports. By minimising the bottlenecks which a drastic shortage of labour would have created, immigration greatly facilitated the flow of cheap foodstuffs and raw materials from the New World to Europe. Furthermore, in speeding the pace of economic development in the various countries of the New World (by lowering the costs of production and enlarging the size of their internal markets for goods and services of all kinds), immigration also increased the ability of primary producing areas to absorb the finished and semi-finished manufactured products which industrialising Europe was able to provide.

If the main problem confronting the economies of the New World was that of labour shortage, the greatest threat to the further development of many agricultural and industrial societies in Europe was that of over-population and labour surplus. On balance, emigration was a considerable advantage to those European countries which contributed most to the stream of emigrants going overseas. Even in England, where the pressure of population growth on the average level of real wages was relatively less severe and where emigration involved the loss of large numbers of skilled men, the net effect of overseas migration was clearly beneficial. It eased some of the worst social and economic problems which high rates of demographic increase had helped to cause, particularly during the period of relative economic depression in the last quarter of the century. Migration was a valuable outlet for those who were unable to find regular work at home, for those displaced by the march of technological progress, and for those who were simply dissatisfied with their present limited opportunities.

Over and above the stimulus it gave to the development of the international economy, rapid population growth, by directly strengthening the domestic economy, made it that much easier for English businessmen to take advantage of the new overseas opportunities offered to them. As R. and K. Titmuss wrote:

Most economists hold that rapidly increasing population in the nineteenth century was a vitally important factor in raising the demands for capital and thereby promoting employment. In assessing, said Mr J. M. Keynes (*Eugenics Review*, XXIX, 1937), the causes of the enormous increase in capital during the nineteenth century and since, too little importance has been given to the influence of an increasing population. This process had, too, an important psychological aspect. In the nineteenth century businessmen never doubted that population and markets would expand. . . . They were able to look ahead and plan ahead in terms of an ever-increasing number of consumers. For them prosperity . . . stretched ahead as far as the eye could see. This optimistic belief . . . led them to expand their plants, take risks, and generally behave in an expansionist manner, thus continually creating new avenues for employment. Increased employment led to increasing consumption which led to more employment and so on (R. and K. Titmuss, *Parents' Revolt*, 1942).

To the extent that the performance of the domestic economy was directly improved by population growth at home its export sectors were better able to respond to the challenges and opportunities afforded by the rapid increase in overseas demand for their goods and services.

The corollary of the view that high rates of demographic increase throughout the period from the late eighteenth to the early twentieth centuries brought nothing but good to the English economy was the belief that decreasing rates of population growth after the First World War were largely responsible for the severe problems which beset the economy in the inter-war years. An extensive quotation from E. C. Snow best illustrates what were once believed to be the effects of demographic retardation on the growth rate of the international economy during the 1920s and 1930s:

In the pre-war period we adjusted our commercial and industrial machinery to provide for an annual increase of about 2 per cent in our total food supplies, and this necessitated an annual increase of about 5 per cent in our imports of foodstuffs. Between 1911 and 1926, however, our total consumption of foodstuffs (by weight) increased by less than $\frac{1}{4}$ per cent per annum, and the highly complicated commercial and industrial machinery which we set up on the basis of requiring an increase of 5 per cent per annum in our imported food supply is only required to produce an annual increase of less than 1 per cent. This simple fact seems to me to be at the bottom of many of the world's economic troubles. Australia and Argentina, for example, two of the countries which have supplied us with enormous quantities of foodstuffs, have organized themselves in the post-war period to expand their production more or less at the same rate as in the pre-war period. . . . If we could have taken more foodstuffs and raw materials from the rest of the world in the past few years, not only would our own exports have been better maintained, but the international trade of other countries would, in turn, have been improved (E. C. Snow, *Journal of the Royal Statistical Society*, XCVIII, 1935).

Because Western European demand for the food and raw material exports of the New World slowed down in the face of demographic retardation, primary producing countries were thus unable to expand their demand for European manufactured products at the rate which had been common before the First World War. Given its relatively heavy dependence on exports, the unfortunate effects of demographic retardation on the growth of international trade had particularly serious consequences for the English economy. What was urgently required in the 1920s and 1930s was a wholesale transfer of resources away from those industries which were producing largely for overseas markets towards those catering for a more stable, protected, domestic demand.

Even at the best of times such a dramatic change of direction was bound to prove extremely difficult. But, so the argument runs, the problems of readjustment were compounded, *inter alia*, by the slowness with which the population of England itself was growing. At precisely the time when the English economy needed to be at its most flexible to combat the serious economic disorders of the inter-war years it was instead rather less adaptable than it had been at any stage throughout the previous century; and, it is argued, low rates of population growth were chiefly to blame for this. The argument was clearly expressed by Professor Titmuss. Because the twentieth-century decline in the pace of demographic increase was due to falling levels of fertility, it was accompanied by a gradual ageing of the population. Not only did the total size of the labour force grow more slowly than it had done in the past, but its average age also rose steadily. As a result the labouring population was less capable of adjusting to meet the constantly changing calls for new skills, less willing to move into new jobs and new areas, and less likely to produce from its ranks those individuals who were equipped to become the entrepreneurs, managers and skilled technicians without whom substantial economic readjustments were impossible. At the same time, just as high rates of population growth in the nineteenth century had increased the size of the domestic market for manufactured goods, so lower rates of population growth in the 1920s and 1930s hindered the further expansion of domestic demand, reduced the profitability of new capital outlays, and restricted the general level of entrepreneurial activity. The inevitable outcome of all this was a slump in the overall pace of economic growth, persistently high levels of unemployment, and an economy which was far less flexible and far less dynamic than it would otherwise have been.

Of course, none of the scholars who subscribed to the view summarised above from the work of Snow and Titmuss was so naïve as to claim that demographic change was solely reponsible for shaping the pace and pattern of English economic development during the nineteenth and twentieth centuries. Economic 'take-off' in the decades after 1780, the sustained growth and diversification of the economy throughout the nineteenth century, the emergence of a truly international economy and Britain's long dominance of it, and, finally, the economic crisis of the inter-war years can only properly be explained by reference to a wide variety of factors. What is significant about the Snow-Titmuss line, however, is the relatively heavy weight attached to one of these factors—population, and the insistence that the long-term achievements of the economy were closely and positively correlated with the pace of population increase; that, in other words, the maintenance of high rates of population growth through the nineteenth century was, on balance, a positive stimulant to economic progress, whereas the decline in rates of population increase during the inter-war period contributed powerfully to economic retardation and dislocation.

*   *   *

The question remains; is the real story quite so straightforward? We did, after all, begin this chapter by looking briefly at the nature of the *theoretical* rôle of population change in economic development. Two points from that discussion are worth recalling at this stage. Firstly, the demographic variable is not the only determinant of the level of effective demand. Variations in per capita real incomes (themselves only partly a reflection of population change) and in the pattern of consumer tastes also exert an influence on the size of the market, especially among populations living comfortably above minimum subsistence standards (as was the population of England for much of the period under consideration). Secondly, although there is a close correlation between population and the size of the labour force, the economic consequences of variations in the number of producers are not easily predictable; in certain circumstances a large and rapidly growing labour force may not foster economic expansion, nor need a small and slowly growing labour force always contribute to economic retardation. In view of these theoretical considerations can we accept the Snow-Titmuss line without a rather closer look at the evidence? Were high rates of population increase quite such an unequivocal blessing to the performance of the English economy in the nineteenth and early twentieth centuries? Was the decline in the rate of population growth after the First World War quite so damaging to the economy as was once believed? Let us first consider in more detail the suggested relationship between population and economic growth in the period of rapid demographic expansion through the nineteenth century to the outbreak of the First World War.

Except for a very brief period in the late eighteenth and early nineteenth centuries when some factory owners continued to have difficulty attracting enough skilled labour, English manufacturing industry invariably had a sufficient supply of labour for its needs. Not even the loss of large numbers of young men to emigration overseas in the latter part of the nineteenth century altered this fact. The ratio of occupied persons to the total population of occupiable age changed little in the forty years or so before the outbreak of the First World War, while in absolute terms the total occupied population rose from 10.3 to 16.3 million between 1871 and 1911. Whatever its other failings the English economy in the period from 1780 to 1911 was not hindered by any shortage of labour. On the contrary, it has been suggested by Professor Habakkuk (*American and British Technology in the*

Nineteenth Century, 1962) that the long-term success of the economy was seriously hampered by an *overabundance* of labour.

Thus, according to Professor Habakkuk, one of the most striking contrasts between the relative experience of American and British industry in the nineteenth century was the eagerness with which American manufacturers seized on labour- and capital-saving technology. In Habakkuk's opinion the basic explanation for this difference stemmed from the fact that American businessmen were perpetually short of labour. Labour scarcity encouraged a search for labour-saving innovations—a search which met little opposition from organised labour unions because it did not threaten the displacement of workers by machines (on the contrary it was likely to result in an increase in the aggregate demand for labour, and a general rise in the level of real wages). Technical progress in one sector of the economy stimulated similar innovations in other sectors, the more so in the American case since any sectoral rise in real wages due to technical progress put pressure on other branches of the economy to introduce labour-saving equipment in order to prevent a drain of labour towards higher income employments. In contrast, in England where labour was in adequate supply, the adoption of labour-saving machinery was less immediately necessary, and more likely to meet strong opposition from workers who saw their livelihoods threatened. Furthermore, in a situation where labour is plentiful, technical developments in one industry are much less likely to denude other industries of their labour supplies. Finally, because the shortage of labour exerted an upward pressure on the level of wages and hence a downward pressure on profit margins, American businessmen also had a particular incentive to introduce capital-saving technology in order to economise on the rising real costs of other factors of production. If an insufficiency of labour ever encouraged a search for labour- and capital-saving machinery in England it could only have done so during the eighteenth century. After the Napoleonic Wars, and throughout the nineteenth and early twentieth centuries, the maintenance of high rates of population growth provided English entrepreneurs with an abundant and elastic labour supply. Although this fostered further investment and innovation within the existing range of techniques and organisation, and thus contributed to high rates of economic growth in the short-run, it positively discouraged the invention and widespread adoption of those labour- and capital-saving devices which were to form the basis of American technological superiority later on. Already by the last quarter of the nineteenth century the damaging effects of labour 'surplus' on the pace of technological innovation were making themselves felt. Technological inferiority was already a major reason for the poor performance of the British economy relative to the economies of its main competitors; and the problems of technological retardation inherited by the inter-war economy were to prove extremely difficult to solve.

Such, in the crudest of terms, is Professor Habakkuk's hypothesis. If it is correct then it goes a long way towards destroying the traditional assumptions set out earlier in this chapter that the existence of an abundant supply of labour was one of the strong points of the English economy in the nineteenth and early twentieth centuries. But *is* it acceptable? Recent criticisms have done much to weaken Habakkuk's case. Indeed, after considering Professor Saul's illuminating conclusion, it is doubtful if any part of it survives at all. *If* British industry was suffering from general technological inferiority in the decades before the First World War (and this remains to be adequately demonstrated) it has still to be proven that the labour factor was in any way responsible. One point raised by Professor Habakkuk has, however, survived unchallenged; namely that an economy like that of the United States was able to expand rapidly (more rapidly than economies where labour supplies were abundant) despite labour shortages and high labour costs. We must assume from this that by the nineteenth century the size of the labour force in industrialising societies was not quite such a vital determinant of the pace of economic growth as Professor Titmuss and others once believed. With industrial growth well under way it mattered much less that England should be blessed by abundant supplies of cheap labour than it had done in the eighteenth century, before industrial 'take-off' and during the early days of the Industrial Revolution. Machines could now more easily be made to do the work of men. It follows therefore that the emphasis attached by earlier writers to the part played by a large supply of cheap labour in the success of the English economy during the nineteenth and early twentieth centuries was clearly exaggerated.

Professor Habakkuk's study serves a valuable corrective purpose in reminding us of this, even though it fails to prove that the pace of English economic growth was actually retarded by an overabundance of labour.

What then of the other traditional assumption—that high rates of population increase through the period from the late eighteenth to the early twentieth centuries formed the basis of a steady expansion in the aggregate size of the market for goods and services of all kinds? How well has this belief stood the test of time?

As previously noted, in theory a growing population is not by itself sufficient to guarantee a rise in the aggregate level of demand. If the rate of population growth outruns the supply of foodstuffs and basic raw materials, average real incomes will fall and the effective market for the wider range of industrial products and commercial services might well decline. In the period between 1750 and 1780, and again from 1850 down to the outbreak of the First World War, the rate of population increase generally kept within, or at least near to, the pace at which additional food and raw material supplies could be made available; before 1780 for reasons we have already discussed; after 1850 principally because of large-scale imports from the primary-producing countries. At worst, the average level of real incomes remained stable in the thirty-year period before 1780. After 1850 it undoubtedly rose, though this is not to deny that large sections of the labouring population continued to live in poverty and unemployment (see George J. Barnsby, 'The standard of living in the Black Country during the nineteenth century', *Economic History Review*, XXIV, 2, 1971), or that many others dissipated a high proportion of their earnings on drink (see A. E. Dingle, 'Drink and working-class living standards in Britain, 1870–1914', *Economic History Review*, XXV, 4, 1972). In both periods, therefore, the continued rapid growth of the population acted as a further stimulus to the size of the domestic market for secondary and tertiary products.

But what happened in the years between 1780 and 1850? Was the initial phase of the 'population revolution' accompanied by a substantial increase in the size of the domestic market? Unquestionably, the level of domestic demand rose during the late eighteenth and first half of the nineteenth centuries if for no other reasons than because the number and purchasing power of 'middle-class' consumers continued to increase. But whether it rose rapidly or not depends very much on what was happening to the level of effective demand among the labouring classes of the population.

Most historians would agree that average per capita real earnings among the English working classes declined in the period from the mid-1790s to the early 1820s. Thereafter, from 1820 to 1850, if they rose at all, the rise was at best only marginal. How, at a time when the economy as a whole was expanding so quickly, do we explain this deterioration in real income standards? Many factors were involved. To begin with, much of the increased output generated by the early Industrial Revolution was absorbed by reinvestment in the capital equipment required for the further development of the industrial economy. Much also was lost to the consumer in the heavy and relatively unproductive expenditures associated with the French wars. The war itself caused serious economic strains and dislocations, the effects of which lasted into the immediate post-war period. When all this is combined with the problems faced by large groups of handicraft workers in their competition with factory production, with the worsening in England's terms of trade between 1815 and 1845, with the material difficulties and social tensions caused by the breakdown of traditional family and village life in manufacturing areas, and with the enormous problems of housing, sanitation and food supply associated with the pace of urbanisation, we go a long way towards explaining the pressure on popular real incomes at a time of rapid overall economic growth. There is, however, one other explanation which must not be overlooked— the high rate at which population was increasing. The vast up-surge in the pace of population growth during the early nineteenth century, in the period before the great influx of primary products from the New World, temporarily outran the rate at which additional food supplies could be expanded to cope adequately with it. This greatly aggravated the relative decline in real wage levels. Even so, the fact that the real incomes of the labouring population were unusually low in the half century prior to 1850 does not mean, of course, that aggregate working-class demand for manufactured products actually decreased. On the contrary, it undoubtedly rose; partly because the absolute number of consumers increased as population grew; partly also because most individuals, even in the period of greatest strain between the mid-1790s and 1820, still had a margin of income for expenditure on non-food goods, albeit a much smaller margin than had been the case for much of the eighteenth century. But—and this is the crux of the present argument—it is likely that the ability of the working class to purchase manufactured goods (and hence the total size of the domestic market) would have been greater in 1850 had the rate of population increase (and hence the pressure on real wages) between 1780 and 1850 been somewhat lower. It is no accident that the major source of demand for the products of many English industries in the late eighteenth and early nineteenth centuries came from overseas.

In the light of more recent research, what therefore still remains of the traditional interpretation, formulated in the 1930s and 1940s, which equated the success of the English economy in the nineteenth and early twentieth centuries with the maintenance of high rates of population growth? No one has ever seriously questioned the long-standing belief that the rapid growth of European population played an integral part in the emergence of a flourishing international economy, from which Britain gained so much. The provision of labour for the economies of the New World and the expansion of overseas demand for the primary goods they produced were both closely dependent on the continuation of high rates of European demographic increase. Rather more questionable is the argument typified above by quotations from the work of Keynes and Titmuss that the rapid growth of England's population acted as a further, and this time a direct, stimulus to the development of the home economy by guaranteeing a large, flexible labour force and a constantly rising level of domestic demand for goods and services. We may not wish to go as far as Professor Habakkuk in suggesting that an overabundance of labour was one of the factors which positively retarded the pace of technological innovation and ultimately lessened the ability of the British economy to withstand external competition. But, if the American case is any indication, we must at the very least question the whole idea that a large and rapidly growing labour supply played a crucial part in facilitating Britain's nineteenth-century economic achievements. Titmuss, Keynes and most of their contemporaries, quite understandably in an age which was being driven frantic by the fear of future depopulation, over-emphasised the contribution of an abundance of labour to economic growth in industrial societies. They were also perhaps rather too sanguine about the relationship between population growth and rising domestic demand during the hundred years or so before 1914. Although this is highly debatable, there are grounds for believing that the home market would have expanded more rapidly if the rate of population growth had been somewhat slower, at least in the period between 1780 and 1850.

Finally, what of the traditional belief that many of the severe problems confronting the English economy in the inter-war period stemmed directly from the sharp downturn in rates of population increase? To what extent was a thriving world economy brought crashing into ruins by falling rates of population growth in Western Europe? How far was the ability of the British economy to adjust successfully to the problems posed by international depression really weakened by retardation in domestic rates of population increase during the 1920s and 1930s?

The enormity of the world's economic problems in the inter-war period is illustrated by the pattern of international trade. As Dr Hobsbawm (*Industry and Empire*, London, 1968) has pointed out, the value of world trade in primary products slumped so drastically that by the years 1936–38 primary-producing countries were able to buy only two-thirds of what they had been able to afford in 1913, and only one-third of what had been within their reach in the period 1926–29. At the same time, and partly as a direct result, the value of world trade in manufactured goods, after having painfully regained its 1913 level by 1929, then fell by a half in the depths of world depression during the early 1930s, and had still not quite recovered its pre-depression peak even as late as 1939.

At the root of many of the world's economic problems lay a persistent imbalance between the supply of, and demand for, foodstuffs and raw materials. Clearly, one part of the explanation for this was the relatively slow pace at which Europe's population grew. Had the total population of Western Europe increased more quickly, so too would its demand for primary products. In turn, primary producing countries would have found it that much easier to expand their purchases of British manufactures and 'invisible' services at something like the old rate. We must not, however, exaggerate the rôle of demographic stagnation in the depression of the inter-war years. The chronic imbalance between the supply of, and demand for, primary products was not due solely, or even primarily, to declining rates of population growth, but rather to an enormous increase in the productivity and output of the world's primary producing industries—the result of sweeping technological and organisational innovations. Moreover, as Professor Landes (*The Unbound Prometheus*, Cambridge University Press, 1969) has argued, if low rates of population growth and relative stagnation in the demand for primary products were really the main sources of difficulty why did the level of trade between the various countries of Europe suffer almost as much as that between Europe and overseas territories? The truth of the matter is that the economic debacle of the inter-war world had its origins in the late nineteenth century *when, significantly, rates of population growth were still extremely high*, and quite obviously involved much more than the meanderings of demography alone. Long before the outbreak of the First World War the era of multilateral free trade, if it ever really existed, was giving way to monopoly and protectionism. Many of Britain's staple export industries were already engaged in a dire and losing struggle against overseas competition. The State was already beginning to intervene in matters previously regarded as the prerogative of private enterprise or the free play of the market. All these developments, which were themselves the logical outcome of the changing nature of the industrial world, were accelerated by the events of the Great War and its immediate aftermath. The most therefore that can be claimed for the rôle of demographic stagnation in the inter-war period is that in a very modest way it contributed to the continuation of economic trends which had long been underway. The plight of the international economy would certainly have been less serious had the population of Europe grown more rapidly, *but only marginally so*. We should avoid attaching too much importance to the part played by the demographic variable in the economic ills of the inter-war years.

Lastly, how acceptable is the belief that declining rates of population growth made it more difficult for the English economy to respond successfully to the new external difficulties facing it in the 1920s and 1930s? To what extent was the pace of domestic economic growth and the much-needed process of economic diversification directly retarded by the fact that demographic deceleration led to shortages of labour and a tightening of the internal market for the products of Britain's 'new' (as opposed to the traditional, export-oriented) industries?

Whatever contemporary writers believed, any suggestion that the labour force was too small to meet the needs of the domestic economy in the inter-war period is palpably absurd. Although the average annual increments to the size of the labour force were smaller than they had been in the second half of the nineteenth century, they were nevertheless far too large to be absorbed by a flagging economy, as the frightening levels of unemployment clearly indicate. Even the new industries had an ample reservoir of labour to call on. Nor is there any reason to suppose that the relatively small annual increase in the aggregate number of producers was accompanied by a decline in the flexibility and efficiency of the work force. To judge from evidence relating to inter-regional migration in the 1920s and 1930s, the ability and willingness of people to move from one area to another in search of work was at least as great, and probably greater, than ever before. Furthermore, with better standards of nutrition and medical care, and longer periods of education and vocational training, the mental and physical qualities of new entrants to the labour force were undoubtedly much higher than those of earlier generations. If there were any problems caused by the decline in the rate at which the labour force expanded, these were probably countered by the fact that workers were better equipped than ever before to meet the increasingly complex demands of an industrial economy.

One of the most striking features of the economic history of the inter-war years was the gradual build-up of a large home market for the products of Britain's 'new' industries—the only ray of light in an otherwise depressingly grim story. It was largely on the fortunes of 'new' industries like housebuilding, household appliances, electrical and chemical goods, motor cars etc., that the painstaking recovery of the economy from depression after 1932 was to be based. In complete contrast to the views formulated in the 1930s which have been set out above, the growth of a home market, and thus the recovery and diversification of the economy, owed a good deal to the very fact that rates of population increase were relatively low.

Historians have always had difficulty in explaining why, in an age of mass unemployment, the average level of per capita real incomes (and with it the size of the domestic market) actually rose. No doubt a variety of factors were involved—improving terms of trade, the rising proportion of salaried employees in the working population, higher standards of labour productivity, narrower income differentials, and so on. But to a large extent the explanation was a demographic one. In the first place declining rates of population growth after the First World War were accompanied by significant alterations in the age-structure of English society. As will be discussed more fully in the following chapter the percentage of the total population below the age of fifteen years decreased, while that in the 'working' age-groups (i.e. 15–64 years) rose. Despite a slight increase in the proportion of 'elderly' persons (i.e. over 64 years of age), the number of 'producers' per 'consumer' increased, and the ratio of the 'dependent' population fell. According to the Report of the Royal Commission on Population (1949) the number of people aged between fifteen and sixty-four years per consumer rose from 0.60 to 0.68 in the period 1891–1947. Between 1911 and 1938 the number of 'producer units' rose by 27% and the number of 'consumer units' by a mere 18% (S. Pollard, *The Development of the British Economy, 1914–1950*, London, 1963). Herein is one of the basic explanations for the gradual rise in per capita real wages during the inter-war period upon which the expansion of the domestic market and the growth of the 'new' industries were largely dependent.

The second facet of demographic change in the inter-war period having significant economic consequences was the steady decline in the average size of families and the relatively rapid increase in the number of separate family or household units which accompanied it. The mean average number of live births per married woman fell from 5.71 for women marrying between 1841 and 1845 to 3.37 for those marrying between 1900 and 1909, and to 2.19 for marriages celebrated between 1925 and 1929. Over the same period the mean size of the domestic household group also declined sharply, from 4.73 in 1851 to 3.72 in 1931 (P. Laslett, 'Size and structure of the household in England over three centuries', *Population Studies*, XXIII, 2, 1969). The total number of 'separate occupiers' (families) in England and Wales rose from 5 million in 1871, to 8 million in 1911, and 10 million in 1931—an increase of 100% over the whole period and of 25% between 1911 and 1931; by comparison the population of England and Wales grew by only 76% and 11% respectively (D. C. Marsh, *The Changing Social Structure of England and Wales, 1871–1961*, London, 1965).

The economic effects of these alterations in the size and number of families were extremely important. Firstly, because small families spent a relatively low proportion of their income on basic subsistence commodities they had a larger margin for expenditure on the less essential goods and services which the 'new' industries were providing. Secondly, as family size declined and births came to be increasingly concentrated in the early years of married life, married women found it easier to take up full-time employment outside the home. The result was a rise in the average level of real family incomes, and a further expansion in the size of the domestic market for manufactured goods. Thirdly, it is worth emphasising that the rapid increase in the number of separate family units during the inter-war period was one of the main reasons for the boom in housebuilding—a boom which was a cause as well as an effect of Britain's recovery from depression after 1932.

Our conclusions about the economic effects of relative demographic stagnation in the 1920s and 1930s must, therefore, be somewhat different from the more pessimistic view favoured by earlier writers. On the one hand the contribution made by lower rates of European population growth to the world's economic problems in the period between the wars was, we believe, greatly exaggerated by the traditional interpretation. On the other, there seems no reason to assume that the efficiency of Britain's domestic economy was in any way seriously impaired by low rates of population growth at home. On the contrary, quite the reverse is suggested by a closer look at the evidence. The trouble with the interpretation typified in the work of Professors Snow and Titmuss was that it was too willing to accept population retardation as a force for economic evil, and not willing enough to consider it as a force for economic good.

* * *

How, finally, might we summarise the part played by population in English economic development since the beginning of the eighteenth century? Two broad conclusions seem to be worth emphasising. Firstly, the influence exerted by the population variable on the pattern of economic growth was undoubtedly much greater in the earlier part of our period, that is, during the eighteenth century, than it was to be later on. As technologies progress and standards of life rise, the rôle of population as the main determinant of productive and consuming power decreases. Secondly, and here we might draw a parallel with the views expressed recently by Professor Chambers (*Population, Economy and Society in Pre-industrial England*), the economic consequences of variations in the rates of population growth are by no means clear-cut. In general, there has been a striking positive correlation between variations in the pace of demographic increase on the one hand and variations in the pace of economic advance on the other. Thus, high rates of population growth from the mid-eighteenth to the early twentieth centuries were associated with, and partly responsible for, industrial 'take-off' and sustained rapid economic advance. Lower rates of population growth in the first half of the eighteenth century and in the 1920s and 1930s were associated with, and again partly responsible for, relative economic stagnation. But in reality the full story is not quite so simple. Tentatively, it is possible to suggest that the nineteenth-century English economy might have been even more successful had rates of population growth been a *little* lower than they were. More convincingly, one might argue that periods of relatively slow population growth have in many respects helped to broaden and stabilise the economy and to prepare the way more surely for subsequent economic advance. At no stage have the economic consequences of demographic change been wholly good or wholly bad. They have, however, always been worthy of note.

FURTHER READING

Books and Monographs

J. D. Chambers, 'The Vale of Trent, 1670–1800', *Economic History Review*, Supplement 3.

J. D. Chambers, *Population, Economy and Society in Pre-industrial England*, Oxford University Press, 1972.

J. D. Chambers and G. E. Mingay, *The Agricultural Revolution, 1750–1880*, London, 1966.

P. Deane and W. A. Cole, *British Economic Growth, 1688–1959*, 2nd ed., Cambridge University Press, 1971.

H. J. Habakkuk, *American and British Technology in the Nineteenth Century*, Cambridge University Press, 1962.

H. J. Habakkuk, *Population Growth and Economic Development since 1750*, Leicester University Press, 1971.

E. L. Jones, *Agriculture and Economic Growth in England, 1750–1815*, London, 1967, especially the Introduction.

W. A. Lewis, *Economic Survey, 1919–1939*, 1st ed., London, 1949, Chapter XIII.

Royal Commission on Population, *Report*, HMSO, London, 1949.

S. B. Saul, *Technological Change: The United States and Britain in the Nineteenth Century*, London, 1970.

B. Thomas, *Migration and Economic Growth. A Study of Great Britain and the Atlantic Economy*, Cambridge University Press, 1954.

B. Thomas (ed.), *The Economics of International Migration*, London, 1958.

R. and K. Titmuss, *Parents' Revolt*, London, 1942, Chapter V.

United Nations, *The Determinants and Consequences of Population Trends*, New York, 1943.

Articles

J. D. Chambers, 'Enclosure and labour supply in the Industrial Revolution', *Economic History Review*, 2nd ser., V, 1953.

D. E. C. Eversley, 'The Home Market and Economic Growth in England', in E. L. Jones and G. E. Mingay (eds.), *Land, Labour and Population in the Industrial Revolution*, London, 1967.

D. E. C. Eversley, 'Population, economy and society', in D. V. Glass and D. E. C. Eversley (eds.), *Population in History*, London, 1965.

M. W. Flinn, 'Agricultural productivity and economic growth: a comment', *Journal of Economic History*, XXVI, 1966.

H. J. Habakkuk, 'Second thoughts on British and American technology in the nineteenth century', *Business Archives and History*, III, 1963.

H. J. Habakkuk, 'Population problems and European economic

development in the late eighteenth and nineteenth centuries', *American Economic Review*, LIII, *Papers and Proceedings*.

A. H. John, 'Aspects of English economic growth in the first half of the eighteenth century', *Economica*, N.S., 28, 1961.

A. H. John, 'Agricultural productivity and economic growth in England, 1700–1760', *Journal of Economic History*, XXV, 1965.

E. L. Jones, 'Agriculture and economic growth in England 1660–1750: Agricultural change', *Journal of Economic History*, XXV, 1965.

J. M. Keynes, 'Some economic consequences of a declining population', *The Eugenics Review*, XXIX, 1, 1937.

J. J. Spengler, 'Demographic factors and early modern economic development', *Daedalus*, 1968.

E. C. Snow, 'The limits of industrial employment (II). The influence of growth of population on the development of industry', *Journal of the Royal Statistical Society*, XCVIII, Part II, 1935.

B. Thomas, 'Migration and the rhythm of economic growth, 1830–1913', *Manchester School of Economic and Social Studies*, XIX, 3, 1951.

6. *Population and Society*

Perhaps it is appropriate that the most perplexing and least considered aspect of the population question should be left to the last. The difficulties involved in trying to describe the intricate relationship between population and the economy or in trying to isolate the principal socio-cultural determinants of population trends are daunting enough. But they are relatively minor by comparison with those we face in attempting to analyse the ways in which the population variable has helped to shape the evolution of modern English society—its structure,* attitudes and actions.

One problem is simply whether or not we have any right to regard population as an autonomous causal agent of cultural, political and social change at all. It can after all be argued that the basic characteristics of any society, including its demographic structure, are determined primarily by the nature of its economy. If this is true then it is to the process of economic change that we should turn for our explanations of the main cultural, social and political features of any population group.

We have, however, previously suggested, following the argument recently developed by Professor Chambers (*Population, Economy and Society in Pre-industrial England*), that at least until the eighteenth century the rhythm and character of population growth was not determined by economic factors or human actions alone. Given that, in the pre-industrial world, population trends were fashioned largely by the 'exogenous forces of nature' they therefore acted as agents of economic change in their own right. And, in theory anyway, there is no reason to suppose that they did

---

*Defined by Professor Marsh as 'those aspects of social life associated with the composition, distribution and divisions of the population which are capable of quantitative measurement' (D. C. Marsh, *The Changing Social Structure of England and Wales, 1871–1961*, London, 1965).

not exert an independent influence over the structure, attitudes and actions of society also.

In the course of industrialisation and economic development the population variable has undoubtedly lost much of its autonomy and a good deal of its relative significance. Demographic trends have become much less dependent on the uncontrollable vagaries of nature and much more dependent on human control; and population itself has become much less vital an agent of economic change than it was in the pre-industrial world. Yet despite this we would be well advised to continue treating the population factor as a potential force for social change. For one thing, although its influence has greatly diminished, even in the most advanced society population still exercises some independent influence on the patterns of economic development, and presumably therefore on the forms of social, cultural and political life too. For another, a thorough appreciation of the rôle of the population factor undoubtedly helps us towards a clearer understanding of the ways in which economic change—arguably the most important determinant of social change in the modern world—reacts on society. After all, it is often through the population processes that variations in the economy act upon the structure and behaviour patterns of a social group. It is, for instance, perfectly true that the rise of trade unionism in nineteenth-century England and the simultaneous changes which occurred in the methods of political franchise were both, at base, the result of economic modernisation. But to fully appreciate why economic growth had such consequences we need to know more about the mechanisms through which it worked. In both cases one such mechanism was population. Thus, the growth of trade unions was partly dependent on the factor of population density; it was possible only when large numbers of people came to live together in urban concentrations. Similarly, electoral reforms were partly dependent on the factor of population migration; they were encouraged by the great changes which had taken place in the geographic distribution of England's population.

Perhaps the greatest difficulty we face in considering the effects of population change on society is that the potential scope of the inquiry is so vast. Professor Sauvy has written that 'demography is not confined to speculations on birth- and death-rates. The variations and distribution of numbers have a strong though discreet influence on all social questions' (A. Sauvy, *General Theory of Population*). If we define the word 'society' in its widest possible sense—to include not only the structure of a population group (that is, its age, sex, household and family composition; its educational, political and religious groupings etc.) but also the attitudes it adopts and the policies it pursues—then the awesome magnitude of our task becomes immediately apparent; because, in one way or another, variations in the size and rate of growth of a population and/or in its vital rates of birth, death and migration have been reckoned to play a significant part in the evolution of social structure, social policies, political organisation, military capacity, cultural values, social psychology, and a good deal more besides.

Thus, English writers on population in the 1930s and 1940s were not concerned simply with the economic consequences of demographic change. They devoted almost as much of their attention to its possible non-economic effects.

How would the future pattern of population growth affect Britain's traditional status as a major power in world politics? Would it make any real difference to the possibility of achieving world-wide political stability? Would it in any way alter the political and cultural relationships between Britain and the Commonwealth?

What is the connection between population and political democracy, or between population and greater centralised control? What will be the political effects of an ageing population? Will, for instance, the processes and decisions of political life become increasingly conservative?

What are the potential psychological, 'emotional' consequences of demographic trends? Do low rates of population growth or, worse, absolute population decline lessen the creative vigour and energy of a society? Does life in a large family more readily breed the virtues of independence, sturdiness and co-operation than life in a small family? Or are rapidly growing and densely crowded populations a source of individual uncertainty, insecurity, tension and mental disorder? What, if any, are the psychological effects of the substitution of impersonal, formalised and institutionalised contacts which large populations necessitate for the close personal relationships which are possible only when populations are small?

How would the relatively rapid decline in rates of fertility among upper- and middle-class groups affect the intellectual and genetic quality of society as a whole? What new social problems emerge as a consequence of population change, particularly of demographic ageing? How do variations in the patterns of fertility, mortality and geographic migration affect the provision of social services like housing, education and health? Will radical changes in social policy be required to cope with them?

Quite clearly a list of questions of this nature and this length poses us several serious problems. We cannot hope to treat them all within the confines of a short chapter like the present. Perhaps this is as well since the range of questions crosses so many different academic disciplines that a thorough discussion of each of them in any case lies far beyond the competence of any one writer. Nor, given the regrettable shortage of detailed work on the effects of population change on society, can we expect to provide any very precise answers even to those questions that we do have time to consider. What follows in this chapter must, therefore, be highly selective and incomplete. It is intended to demonstrate that the demographic variable does have an influence on the structure, attitudes and policies of a society, and to suggest some of the ways in which it does so. It is not, nor could it hope to be, either definitive or all-embracing. We will look first at the influence of population on certain aspects of social structure; then at the nature of the relationship between population and politico-military power; and finally at the part played by population in determining the level of individual well-being and happiness, that is, in determining what we might for purposes of short-hand call the 'rate of social progress'.

1. *Population and Social Structure*

The detailed analysis of regional and chronological variations in the social structure of the population of England and Wales since pre-industrial times has only recently begun. Professor Marsh (*The Changing Social Structure of England & Wales, 1871–1961*) paved the way with his study of the data on age, sex and marital distribution, household and family size, occupational, educational and religious groupings contained in the published census returns. There is still, however, room for much more work to be done on these returns, both for the period before 1871 when Professor Marsh's study begins and on regional variations in social composition. Furthermore, in spite of its undoubted value, the published census material tells us only part of the story. For example, census information on the average number of persons per household is often not as exact as we might wish; nor does it permit us to study the detailed composition of households—the number of separate family units they contained, the ratio between adult and child members, the frequency with which they were shared by more than two generations, the proportion of households with resident servants, the relationship between the size of the household and the social class of its head, and so on. Moreover, quite apart from the inadequacies of the published returns there is, of course, the problem that official census data do not exist for the period before 1801.

Recognising the limitations of the published returns, students of the history of social structure have latterly turned their attention to other possibilities. For the period after 1841 (though to date only to 1871 when the operation of the one-hundred years rule comes into effect) many of the important questions left unanswered in the published material can be tackled by a careful analysis of the original manuscript returns of the census enumerators, copies of which are available from the Public Record Office. For the period before 1841 * a similar, albeit less detailed and less extensive, analysis can be attempted on the basis of data contained in the better quality local listings of inhabitants that have survived.

At present, there are unfortunately few completed studies based on enumerators' books and inhabitants' listings available to us.†

---

*Less detailed census enumerators' returns are available for the censuses of 1801, 1811, 1821 and 1831. But only a few local ones seem now to be extant. For further details see *Local Population Studies Magazine and Newsletter*, vol. 2, pp. 53–55; vol. 5, p. 43; vol. 7, pp. 58–60.

†Among those already available P. Laslett and J. Harrison, 'Clayworth and Cogenhoe', in H. E. Bell and R. L. Ollard (eds.), *Historical Essays, 1600–1750*, London, 1963; N. L. Tranter, 'Population and Social Structure in a Bedfordshire parish', *Population Studies*, XXI, 3, 1967; C. H. Law, 'Local censuses in the 18th century', *Population Studies*, XXIII, 1, 1969; P. Laslett, 'Size and structure of the household in England over three centuries', *Population Studies*, XXIII, 2, 1969; M. Anderson, *Family*

Most researchers are still chiefly concerned with trying to create the proper procedural, methodological basis for such studies.* Our knowledge of recent changes in the social structure of modern England is therefore far from complete. And consequently we are in no position to undertake a thorough evaluation of the effect that variations in population trends have had upon it.

TABLE VIII *Distribution of the population by age-groups, England and Wales, 1695–1931*

	1695	*1821*	*1871*	*1911*	*1931*
0–9	27.6	27.9	25.4	20.9	15.8
10–19	20.2	21.1	20.3	19.0	16.6
20–29	15.5	15.7	16.7	17.3	17.1
30–39	11.7	11.8	12.8	15.2	14.7
40–49	8.4	9.3	10.1	11.5	13.1
50–59	5.8	6.6	7.3	8.0	11.1
60 and above	10.7†	7.3	7.4	8.0	11.6

Sources: B. R. Mitchell and P. Deane, *Abstract of British Historical Statistics*, Cambridge University Press, 1962.
D. V. Glass, 'Two papers on Gregory King', in D. V. Glass and D. E. C. Eversley (eds.), *Population in History*, London, 1965.

Structure in Nineteenth-century Lancashire, Cambridge University Press, 1971; P. Laslett (ed.), *Household and Family in Past Time*, Cambridge University Press, 1972; R. Smith, 'Early Victorian household structure', *International Review of Social History*, 1970; N. L. Tranter, 'The social structure of a Bedfordshire parish in the mid-nineteenth century', *International Review of Social History*, 1973.

---

*For a discussion of methodology see particularly the relevant chapters in E. A. Wrigley (ed.), *An Introduction to English Historical Demography*, London, 1966; E. A. Wrigley (ed.), *Nineteenth Century Society*, Cambridge University Press, 1972.

†Professor Glass suggests that King's estimate of the proportion of the population aged sixty years and above is rather too high. The data recently derived from the analysis of extant listings of inhabitants appear to confirm his suspicions.

Even so it is quite clear from the somewhat scanty information which does exist that the demographic variable has had a part to play in determining variations in the structure of English society. We can illustrate this by looking briefly at the effect that population trends have had on the alterations which have occurred in age distribution and household size.

Except for his somewhat inflated estimate for the age-group above sixty years, the accuracy of Gregory King's observations has been confirmed by recent research. According to King 47.8% of the population of England and Wales at the end of the seventeenth century was below twenty years of age, while one in every ten persons was at least sixty years old. At Ealing in 1599 the respective proportions were 45.8% and 6.1%; at Stoke-on-Trent in 1701 47.9% and 8.4% (Laslett, *The World we have Lost*); among cottage tenement dwellers at Cardington in 1782 49.8% and 5.3%; at Cardington in 1851 50% and 6.2% (Tranter, *Population Studies*, 1967; *International Review of Social History*, 1973). In general, the age distribution of the English population in the eighteenth century closely resembled that of other populations of North and Western Europe in the same period. In Sweden in 1750 42.3% of the population was below the age of twenty, and 9.7% above the age of sixty; in Finland in 1751 46.9% and 9.1%; in Denmark in 1787 40.4% and 8.7% (H. Gille, Demographic history of the Northern European countries, *Population Studies*, III, 1, 1949); in France around 1775 42.6% and 7.1% (J. Bourgeois-Pichat, 'The general development of the population of France', in Glass and Eversley (eds.), *Population in History*).

As late as 1871 there had been little change in the age distribution of the population of England and Wales. Despite the revolutionary economic and demographic developments of the previous hundred years, the fact is that so long as birth- and death-rates remained high the age-structure continued basically unchanged. Still, 45.7% of the population was aged below twenty years, while only 7.4% lay in the age-group sixty and above.

Since the late nineteenth century and more especially since 1911, however, the age distribution of England's population has undergone a notable transformation. By 1911 the ratio of the population below twenty years of age had fallen to 39.9%, and by 1931 to 32.4%. On the other hand, the proportion of people aged sixty and above had risen to 8.0% by 1911, and to 11.6% by the early

1930s. The factor most responsible for this was the steady fall in the average level of fertility. As crude birth-rates declined so too did the relative size of the youngest age-cohort in the population, in spite of the fact that infant, child and juvenile mortality rates were also declining steadily. Together with the gradual decline in adult mortality, this has led to a significant rise in the average age of England's population and to an age distribution rather more weighted towards the older age-groups.

A second illustration of the way in which population trends have influenced the structure of English society is provided by the history of long-run variations in household size.*

TABLE IX *Mean household size, England and Wales,* 1564–1649 *to* 1951

Period		Period	
1564–1649	5.1	1891	4.6
1650–1749	4.7	1911	4.4
1750–1821	4.5	1921	4.1
1801	4.6	1931	3.7
1851	4.7	1951	3.2

Sources: P. Laslett, 'Size and structure of the household in England over three centuries', *Population Studies*, XXIII, 2, 1969.
J. W. Nixon, 'Comments on Peter Laslett's paper', *Population Studies*, XXIV, 3, 1970.
P. Laslett, 'A comment on J. W. Nixon's note', *Population Studies*, XXIV, 3, 1970.

Although we might wish for rather more information on the period before 1801, the long-run trend in the average size of the domestic group is clear enough. Until the late nineteenth century or, more noticeably, until the period between the world wars the mean size of the English household altered hardly at all. From the sixteenth and early seventeenth centuries down to the opening of

---

*Mr Laslett defines the household or domestic group as 'that unit or block of persons which was recognised by pre-industrial Englishmen to be distinct from other units or blocks of persons when the inhabitants of a community were listed' (Laslett, *Population Studies*, XXIII, 2, 1969).

the present century each household unit contained on average between four and a half and five persons, usually in two generations. Thus, throughout the long period from 1574 to 1821 70.4% of all households in England and Wales contained parents and their immediate offspring only. In all, the staggering figure of 94.1% of all household units were comprised of one or two generations (Laslett, *Population Studies*, XXIII, 2, 1969). The large households cluttered with grandparents, other relations and hordes of retainers, which were supposedly typical of pre-industrial times are clearly mythical, found perhaps only among the very highest income groups.*

Within this general picture of stability, there were no doubt certain marked regional and chronological differences in the size and structure of the domestic group. Gregory King long ago pointed to the variations which existed between the number of occupants per household in rural and urban areas. Mr Law's recent analysis of extant eighteenth-century listings confirms King's findings. Whereas the average domestic group in villages and small towns contained between four and four and three-quarter persons, that in large towns contained anything between four and a half and six. He goes on to suggest that 'the relationship between persons and houses may be more closely correlated with the rate at which a settlement grows than simply with its size. Thus, the ratio of persons per household in Manchester (six) where the city was expanding rapidly was higher than that at Norwich (five), a larger town, but one that was growing very little' (Law, *Population Studies*, XXIII, 1, 1969).

No doubt too future research will yield abundant examples of populations whose social structure altered significantly between one period and another. In the small Bedfordshire township of Cardington, for example, the proportion of households which comprised parents and their immediate offspring only apparently declined from 76.9% in 1782 to 53.2% in 1851; and the increasing frequency of 'shared' households which this reflected occurred primarily because the rate of population growth over the first half of the nineteenth century exceeded the rate at which

---

*They do not seem to have been very common outside England either, see P. Laslett (ed.), *Household and Family in Past Time*, Cambridge University Press, 1972.

additional housing stock could be provided (Tranter, *International Review of Social History*, 1973).

Nevertheless, when full allowance is made for regional and chronological differentials, the fact remains that in its basic essentials, the English domestic group changed very little between the sixteenth and early twentieth centuries. Households remained small, and more often than not comprised the nuclear family of man, wife and children only.

Whatever effect the Industrial Revolution had on the relationships and responsibilities of the family and its individual members —and Professor Smelser (*Social Change in the Industrial Revolution*) has shown that the effect was probably considerable—it did not result in any immediate or drastic alteration in the size and composition of the typical household unit. It is interesting to note that even in the highly industrial town of Preston in 1851, although the average number of persons per household was somewhat higher than normal (5.4), almost three-quarters of all households (73%) were made up of man, wife and immediate offspring only (Anderson, *Family Structure in Nineteenth Century Lancashire*).

As was the case with the age-distribution of England's population, a significant and lasting transformation in household size had to await the onset of the secular decline in the average levels of marital fertility which got under way in the late nineteenth and early twentieth centuries. Mr Laslett has drawn our attention to the fact that the slight rise in English net reproduction rates which occurred between 1841 and the 1870s was followed by a temporary recovery in the size of the domestic group during the 1870s and 1880s; whilst the consistent decline in the level of net reproduction rates between the 1880s and the early 1930s (for which declining rates of marital fertility were responsible) was matched, and indeed was largely the cause of, a parallel fall in the mean size of the English household. That the level of reproduction was not entirely responsible for determining the average size of households is, however, quite clear from the fact that whereas the rates of both fertility and net reproduction rose again between the 1930s and the early 1960s the mean size of the domestic group continued to decline (Laslett, *Population Studies*, XXIII, 2, 1969). Clearly, factors other than demographic ones have a part to play. But falling fertility remains an important element in the decline that has occurred in the mean size of the English household in recent generations.

Through its influence on social structure the effect of population change is carried over into the sphere of social policy. Once changes in social structure occur they invariably give rise to the need for wholly new social attitudes and social policies to deal with them. The rapid urbanisation of English society in the nineteenth century, for example, required entirely new areas of state legislation and activity to cope with the terrifying problems resulting from it. Again, the recent fall in the average size of the domestic group coupled with the sharp increase in the number of separate household units since 1911 has necessitated a drastic extension and alteration in society's housing policies. But the clearest, and in many ways the saddest, indication of the link between demography, social structure and the emergence of new social problems is revealed by the consequences of ageing. As both the absolute and relative number of old people in society has increased it has raised a host of social and economic problems. Quite apart from the problem of inadequate incomes, what was to be done about the dilemma of loneliness among the elderly, particularly among elderly widows living alone? What could be done to integrate old people more closely into the day-to-day workings of society, to make them feel that they still had a valuable and meaningful part to play in the world? Could, indeed, an ageing society afford not to utilise the talents and experience which its elderly members possess? None of these problems has yet been completely solved, though we have long been aware of their existence and have gone some way towards their solution.

* * *

Despite the limitations of the available evidence, there can be little doubt that population change has had a part to play in determining the basic features of modern English social structure; and that, through its influence on social structure, the demographic variable has also had a hand in deciding the kind of social problems society has had to face. But it remains a task for future research to determine exactly how significant the rôle of population has been by comparison with that of the other causal influences at work.

2. *Population and Politics*

Much of the emphasis placed by seventeenth- and eighteenth-century writers and statesmen on the need for a large and rapidly growing population followed logically from their belief that a nation's political strength was determined largely by the sheer number of men who could be called to bear arms. John Graunt's urgent plea for a bigger population in the mid-seventeenth century, for example, was occasioned almost solely by political and military considerations—by the uncomplicated assumption that the larger the population the greater would be England's military might (J. Graunt, *Natural and Political Observations . . . Made upon the London Bills of Mortality*, London, 1676).

Later writers did not view the relationship between population size and political power quite so simply. As John Howlett pointed out towards the end of the eighteenth century, Great Britain was militarily weaker than France not simply because her population was smaller. He went on from this to suggest that the political strength of a society depended on more than numerical strength alone (J. Howlett, *An Examination of Dr Price's Essay on the Population of England and Wales*, Maidstone, 1781). Even so, all writers of the period, Howlett among them, remained convinced that the total size of a population was a crucial, if not the only, determinant of political power.

Much the same view continued to prevail throughout the nineteenth and early twentieth centuries. In recent times it received its clearest and most public expression in Mussolini's Ascension Day speech of May 1927:

> What are the 40 millions of Italians as opposed to 90 millions Germans and 200 million Slavs? Let us turn to the West: what are 40 million Italians as opposed to 40 million French, plus the 90 millions in their colonies, or as opposed to the 46 million English, plus the 450 millions in their colonies? To count for something in the world Italy must have a population of not less than 60 millions when she arrives at the threshold of the second half of this century. . . . With a falling population, one does not create an empire but becomes a colony (quoted in D. V. Glass, *Population Policies and Movements in Europe*, London, 1940, reprinted, 1967).

A similarly emotive spirit was in evidence in Britain too. As early as 1920 alarm over the possible dangers inherent in declining rates of fertility had forced the National Birth Rate Commission of that year to conclude that 'in the event of a war similar to that which we have just experienced, what would happen to us with a greatly reduced birth-rate? Surely all we have would be taken, and we must become slaves'.

The continued decline in English birth-rates throughout the inter-war period led to the appearance of much more literature in the same vein. Mrs Hubback's opinions, which we have used before as being typical of her time, are once again illustrative. Quite properly, she begins by stating that 'a country's status and her influence bear no very close relationship to the size of her population'. The strength of a nation's economy, the qualities of her leaders and her men are, she admits, equally important considerations. But she goes on to write:

> If, indeed, its birth-rate were to fall below replacement level, the numbers of men young enough to be among the producing and fighting ages would shrink more than in proportion to the whole population. This position is already clearly visible in this country. We are finding it difficult to secure the 750,000 or so needed for the Forces and our industries are crying out for more workers. It has been reckoned that by the year 2000 the age-group of men between 15 and 35 would, if our pre-war trends continued, number just half what it did in 1939. We would then be bound to become a second- or third-class power. . . . We ourselves should indeed have been in a parlous position during the last war if we had not had the support, not only of the Commonwealth, but also of Allies with far bigger populations than our own.

And again:

> It was a Britain growing more rapidly than other European Powers which built the Empire and became for more than a century the determining factor in world policy. Her growing numbers also enabled the Dominions to be peopled almost entirely from the Mother Country. . . . As things have turned

out, most of the Dominions . . . have population trends much like our own. In relation to their resources they are still underpopulated and are looking to this country to continue to supply them with young people. We, however, shall not have the people—especially the young people—to spare to mitigate their underpopulation. . . . A Britain with a much smaller population would no longer be an important influence in world affairs, either in peace or war; she would lose her status and power, with all that implies as regards the welfare of the Commonwealth and of the world (E. M. Hubback, *The Population of Britain*, London, 1942).

The fears expressed by Mrs Hubback were echoed time and again by countless other authors. Few doubted that an absolute, or even a relative, decline in Britain's population would be accompanied by a loss of her status as a major international power and by the disruption of the Commonwealth, at least in the form in which it then existed.

The idea that a large and growing population was essential to political success was paralleled by a belief that population growth was itself a principal cause of political aggression and expansion. One of the most explicit formulations of this belief is to be found in the work of Harold Cox. In explaining the causes underlying the expansion of the Japanese empire in the late nineteenth and early twentieth centuries, Cox noted that:

Each race as it grows in numbers, and finds increasing need of fresh outlets, seeks those outlets by invading any other territory that is attractive to it. . . . The Japanese people want new markets and new territory because their population is expanding rapidly.

He proceeded to quote similar views widely held by contemporary German writers.

Strong, healthy and flourishing nations increase in numbers. From a given moment they require a continual expansion of their frontiers, they require new territory for the accommodation of their surplus population. Since almost every part of the globe is inhabited, new territory must, as a rule, be obtained at the cost of its possessors—that is to say by conquest, which thus becomes a law of necessity (Von Bernhardi, *Germany and the Next War*, 1911).

We must endeavour to acquire new territories throughout the world by all means in our power, because we must preserve to Germany the millions of Germans who will be born in the future, and we must provide for their food and employment. They ought to be enabled to live under a German sky and to lead a German life (Von Bernhardi, *Unsere Zukunft*, 1912).

From all these assembled views and from what he believed to be the lesson that history taught, Cox, while allowing that 'the causes of war are almost as numerous as human motives', came to the conclusion that 'the growth of population with the resulting desire for economic expansion is a necessary cause of war' (H. Cox, *The Problem of Population*, London, 1922).

By the inter-war period, then, most writers were impelled by their beliefs into what must be one of the most disastrous circular traps imaginable. They were in no doubt that to be successful in war a country needed a large and rapidly multiplying population, and the policies they advocated for encouraging rates of population increase were firmly committed to achieving this objective. Yet, they also realised perfectly well that in stimulating the rate of population growth they were making war and aggression that much more inevitable. Little wonder that Harold Cox advocated the formation of yet another international league, this time a League of Low Birth-Rate Nations, as the only possible hope of breaking out of the vicious circle.

The question arises, however, whether earlier writers were justified in claiming such a close and significant relationship between population and politics. To what extent has population growth really been a cause of political expansion and military aggression? To what extent is the armed strength and political influence of any society dependent on the size and rate of growth of its population? Looking back over history from the vantage point of a calmer and certainly better-informed age we are in a more suitable position to judge than were our predecessors.

Even so, both questions are extremely difficult to answer with any degree of certainty or precision.

The relationship between the size and growth rate of a population on the one hand and its tendency towards forceful aggression on the other is, it must be admitted immediately, by no means straightforward. A large and rapidly growing population will lead to a desire for territorial expansion only if domestic resources cannot cope with the additional demands placed upon them. And even then overpopulation and the consequent need to expand one's territories in the search for food, raw materials or additional 'living-room' need not inevitably result in military conflict with other peoples. There have in history been many instances of nations, forced to expand by the pressure of population at home, that have been able to enlarge their territories quite peacefully either because they have moved into unoccupied lands or because their surplus populations have been easily assimilated into neighbouring societies. There have also been many examples of nations where the most drastic overpopulation has been followed not by a determination to acquire new lands by force if necessary, but rather by a pathetic resignation simply to make the best of the resources they already had. The native population of the Dutch colony of Java, for example, rose from an estimated 10 million in 1800 to 28.3 million in 1900 and to a staggering 47.5 million by 1940 (B. Peper, 'Population growth in Java in the nineteenth century', *Population Studies*, XXIV, 1, 1970). Unquestionably, by the early twentieth century, the pressure of population on resources was severe in the extreme. Yet instead of resulting in a serious political challenge to the dominance of their Dutch masters or even to a large-scale migration of Javanese into the sparsely populated Outer Provinces, the overwhelming bulk of the native population turned quietly inwards and attempted to come to terms with their problems by a more intensive application of the resources and techniques upon which they had long relied (C. Geertz, *Agricultural Involution. Processes of Ecological Change in Indonesia*, Berkeley, 1963).

There have, of course, in the past been numerous cases where wars and forcible expansion do, at first sight, appear to have been associated with overpopulation. Dr Hollingsworth has pointed to the great invasions of people from Asia into Europe between the third and the sixth and again from the twelfth to the fifteenth centuries as excellent illustrations of this. It has frequently been argued that the expansion of European Powers into tropical and sub-tropical lands during the age of so-called New Imperialism in the late nineteenth century is yet another, more recent example. The new areas were required to accommodate Europe's surplus population; to provide new sources of foodstuffs and raw materials to cope with rapidly rising home demand; or as fresh outlets for European investment capital and manufactured products at a time when domestic opportunities were drying up in the face of overpopulation and stagnating consumer real incomes. So at least the argument runs.

When looked at a little more closely, however, one is forced to question the validity of such claims. Take the case of nineteenth-century New Imperialism for example. Whatever the real reasons for this grand theft of territory may have been, it was not to any significant extent caused by the demographic factor. The newly acquired tropical and sub-tropical territories never attracted more than the smallest handful of European immigrants, and only the most marginal amounts of investment capital and manufactured products. Neither did they provide more than a tiny fraction of the food and raw material imports required by European societies. While it is true that Europe's overseas empire could not have been established and maintained without a sufficiently large domestic population to supply the necessary soldiers and administrators, there is no firm evidence to suggest that this empire was the consequence of serious population pressure at home. Most of the emigrants who fled from the overpopulated parts of Europe in the late nineteenth century went not to the newly won tropical colonies but to the long established lands of white settlement, particularly on the North American continent.

In short, then, all that we can say with any certainty about the significance of overpopulation as a cause of war and political conflict is this: that although there have been instances when the pressure of population on domestic resources led directly to forceful aggression, there have been many other cases when for one reason or another it did not. Wars and other acts of aggression can be caused by many things. Overpopulation is certainly one of them, but it would be most unwise to exaggerate its significance. Indeed, as the Javanese experience seems to suggest, the strains arising from an excess population need not always lead to a spirit of aggressiveness. Depending on the circumstances, they might instead give rise to an attitude of hopeless resignation and acceptance. Moreover, if we are to use England's recent experience as our yardstick, then the case for the demographic determination of political and military events becomes weaker still. It would be difficult indeed to demonstrate that the various acts of political aggression which Britain has committed since the eighteenth century were triggered off by the need to cater for the demands of too large a population.

Turning to the second question that we set ourselves: to what extent are political and military successes determined by the size of the population? In the modern industrial world it is patently absurd to assume that there is a simple positive correlation between political strength and population size. The vastness of the population of the Indian sub-continent is not alone enough to raise India to the status of a major international power. Again, one might ask why, if population is a crucial factor in determining military capacity, did the Chinese empire fall easy prey in the late nineteenth and early twentieth centuries to far less populous nations like Britain and Germany, or to its much smaller neighbour Japan? The answer is simply that in the modern industrial world national strength depends on very much more than demographic considerations alone. Admittedly, the sheer size of a population, its sex and age composition, directly determines the number of men available for the armed forces. And the larger this reservoir of manpower is the bigger will be the armies and the easier it will be to make good heavy losses in fighting strength. But ever since the Industrial Revolution these demographic criteria of military might have become increasingly less important. From the early nineteenth century onwards national power has been dependent on productive capacity, that is, on the total size of the national income and on the ability of a society to convert sufficient of this income to produce the most up-to-date weapons of war. In the post-industrial world national strength is primarily a matter of economic and technological sophistication, and only in a very small way of population size. The ease with which Western European nations overran African and Asiatic states in the late nineteenth century was the result of an economic superiority which gave them the military technology to dominate societies the populations of which were sometimes far larger than their own.* If, in the modern world, the most populous among the industrial nations are militarily also the most powerful, this is not because their populations are larger but rather because their economies are the strongest and the most advanced.† English writers in the 1930s and 1940s were quite right to worry about the future decline of England's status as a major international power. But they were quite wrong in believing that this would be the result of demographic retardation. In reality it was to be an inevitable consequence of the decline of her economy relative to that of other states.

In the pre-industrial world, when men rather than machines were much more the basic tools of war (and when in any case population was a more important determinant of economic strength than it was to become in the course of industrialisation), a large and growing population was unquestionably a more vital ingredient in military capacity. But even here we must be careful not to exaggerate its relative importance. It is surely significant that the Manchu conquest and dominance of the vast Chinese empire in the early seventeenth century was achieved against enormous demographic odds. At no stage did the Manchu population of China exceed more than a tiny percentage of the total population of the empire. Obviously, even in the pre-industrial world, the relationship between population and military capacity was not a simple one. The military disadvantages of a small population could be, and frequently were, outweighed by other crucial determinants of national strength—the superior organisation and training of the armed forces, the use of more efficient military tactics, or simply by the fact that the martial spirit, the willingness to fight, may have been more ardent in one nation than another.

We must conclude, therefore, that the relationship between

---

*Indeed, it is worth pointing out that in many of these societies a large and growing population, by retarding the rate of economic development, actually weakened military capabilities.

†Of course, as we saw in an earlier chapter, given the proper circumstances a large and increasing population will stimulate the pace of economic development. But population is only one of the many causes of economic growth, and, in the modern world, an increasingly less important one.

population on the one hand, and political aggressiveness and power on the other is as complex as the relationship between population and other strategic variables. The belief that over-population bred war and political conflict is no doubt justified to a certain extent, especially in the pre-industrial world. But relative to the many other causes of international strife its significance has certainly been exaggerated by earlier writers. Similarly, the belief that political power correlates positively with population size is also true up to a point, again particularly in pre-industrial times. But here too its significance relative to other determinants of national strength seems often to have been overstated. The relationship between population and politics, like that between population and the economy, is undoubtedly meaningful enough to be worth considering. But we must take care to recognise its limitations.

3. *Population and Social Progress*

Considerations of the way in which population change influences social structure and of the relationship between population and politics are really only part of a much broader question which has exercised men's minds from time immemorial—what, if any, is the connection between population growth and social progress? Is population increase a force for social improvement? Does it stimulate the emergence of a better organised society, one in which people are generally more contented? Or, instead, is population growth a potential source of social breakdown and popular misery?

The debate about the effect of population growth on social progress long preceded the appearance of the Reverend Malthus's First Essay on Population in 1798. An early, pessimistic view had been expressed by Sir William Petty in 1682:

Memorandum, That if the People double in 360 Years, that the present 320 Millions computed by some Learned Men, (from the Measures of all the Nations of the World, their degrees being Peopled, and good Accounts of the people in several of them) to be now upon the Face of the Earth, will within the next 2000 Years so increase as to give one Head for every two Acres of Land in the Habitable part of the Earth. And then, according to the Prediction of the Scriptures, there must be Wars and great Slaughter, &c. (W. Petty, *Another essay in Political Arithmetic, concerning the growth of the City of London*, 1683, in C. H. Hull (ed.), *The Economic Writings of Sir William Petty*, Cornell University Press, 1899, Reprints of Economic Classics, 2 vols., New York, 1963).

In general, however, the sympathies of seventeenth- and eighteenth-century writers lay with the opposite view. In 1695, John Cary (*An Essay on the State of England*) took the line that population growth set in motion a process which ultimately led not only to a higher stage of economic development but also to a more satisfactory form of social organisation. Half-a-century later Josiah Tucker, in the same tradition, emphasised the contribution of a large and growing population to economic development, the furtherance of political and social equality, and the promotion of industriousness and good morals.

Where a Country is thinly peopled . . . the greater Part of those few Inhabitants must lead a sauntering, lazy and savage Life, thereby making new Approaches to the State of mere Animals, the most wretched of all others for an human Creature to be in . . . where a Country is thinly peopled . . . the Figure that Commerce can make must be very mean and contemptive . . . the Property of Lands will be the more easily ingrossed, and intailed in a few Families; by which means the Land-holders become more absolute and despotic over their Vassals . . . whereas Commerce, as it is calculated to extend Industry, Happiness and Plenty, equalizes Mankind more than any other Way of Life; and at the same time that it connects them together in Bonds of mutual interest, it renders them FREE. Trade and Vassalage, Commerce and Slavery are, in their Natures, repugnant to each other (J. Tucker, 'The elements of commerce and the theory of taxes', 1755, in R. L. Schuyler (ed.), *Josiah Tucker. A Selection from his Economic and Political Writings*, New York, 1931).

The debate on the potential social consequences of population growth was, however, not hotly joined until Malthus published his famous essay at the close of the eighteenth century.

Although, in reality, Malthus's population theory was never as pessimistic as some of its critics maintained, the essence of the Malthusian contention was, nevertheless, that a growing population, if not carefully controlled, would effectively destroy any real chance of continuous social progress. In responding to what he regarded as William Godwin's wildly utopian visions of the perfectibility of human society Malthus wrote:

> I say, that the power of population is indefinitely greater than the power in the earth to produce subsistence for man. Population, when unchecked, increases in a geometrical ratio. Subsistence increases only in an arithmetical ratio. . . . This natural inequality of the two powers of population, and of production in the earth, and that great law of our nature which must constantly keep their effect equal, form the great difficulty that to me appears insurmountable in the way to the perfectibility of society. . . . I see no way by which man can escape from the weight of this law which pervades all animated nature. . . . And it appears, therefore, to be decisive against the possible existence of a society, all the members of which, should live in ease, happiness and comparative leisure. . . . Consequently, if the premises are just, the argument is conclusive against the perfectibility of the mass of mankind (T. R. Malthus, *First essay on population*, 1798, reprinted for the Royal Economic Society with notes by J. Bonar, London, 1926).

Of course, Malthus was here referring to the possibility of society ever attaining the state of ultimate perfectibility. Elsewhere in his text, he was prepared to allow that the constant imbalance between population and food resources had played a positive rôle in helping to raise mankind above the level of savages if only because the prospects of hunger and starvation induced men to work harder and to make greater efforts to improve their condition. But it is quite clear that Malthus did not see this conflict between population and food resources as being sufficient to generate the continued progress of society upwards and onwards until it finally reached the ultimate state of perfection that Godwin, Condorcet and others had in mind. Long before the final state of perfectibility could be reached, the uneasy balance between population and food supply would have collapsed into a catastrophic food crisis, and society would be cast down towards the savage state once again.

While the Malthusian thesis attracted a good deal of support, particularly during the early part of the nineteenth century, it also met a rising crescendo of criticism. Some writers, like James Grahame, accepted the fact that population always tended to press on the means of subsistence, but were very much more optimistic about the consequences of this than ever Malthus was. Thus, according to Grahame, the real or threatened pressure of population on food resources greatly stimulates man's efforts to produce, and in doing so invariably ensures that mankind always produces enough to feed itself. Additionally, the fact that the upper and middle classes of society will choose to limit their fertility in order to forestall the danger of declining real incomes caused by a possible rise in food prices means that the higher ranks of society can be filled only by greater upward mobility from the lower. The fuller these lower ranks become in the course of population growth, the more intense will be the competition to ascend the social ladder and, from this, the greater will be the benefit to society as a whole (J. Grahame, *An inquiry into the Principle of Population*, Edinburgh, 1816). Other writers, like George Ensor (*An Inquiry Concerning the Population of Nations* . . ., London, 1818) and Archibald Alison (*The Principles of Population and their Connection with Human Happiness*, Edinburgh, 1840), quite simply rejected the notion that population ever in practice pressed on the means of subsistence, and went on to state that a growing population was an essential condition for the advancement of society to a higher stage of civilisation. But one of the fullest and clearest early rejections of the Malthusian thesis can be found in the work of Simon Gray.

The increase of population is, directly, as well as indirectly, the grand permanent source of the increase of wealth, both to individuals and to nations. . . . The increase of population extends and improves the cultivation of the soil, and renders men less dependent on the varieties of the climate. . . . The increase of population tends equally to cultivate and improve the mind of the population as the soil on which it dwells. It has as strong a natural civilizing as it has a fertilizing

influence. ... From wealth spring more polished and luxuri-
ous manners; and it gives rise to a great variety of new
modes of employment, which require skill and cultivation of
the mind. Bringing men more together also, it both increases
their wants and desires, and by means of mutual stimulation
and assistance, enables them to reach a higher process in the
arts and sciences in all their extent. Accordingly, in proportion as a country grows more populous, it grows more
civilized. ... On examining the history of man from the
earliest period of his existence which is at all known, we
find the history of the progress of population to be the
history of the progress of civilization. ... The length of time
required to civilize or decivilize a people depends chiefly on
the rate of increase or decrease of the population (S. Gray,
The Happiness of States . . ., London, 1815).*

One way or another, therefore, eighteenth- and nineteenth-
century writers were convinced that variations in the size and
rate of growth of a population exercised an important influence
on the pace of social progress. Some considered the population
factor to be a force for improvement, others, like Malthus,
regarded population as a serious potential hindrance to social
advancement. In the period between the world wars, as Malthusian fears of overpopulation receded, most English authors
and statesmen believed that a growing population was highly
desirable; that it was essential to the attainment of a materially
wealthier and emotionally more satisfying life.

Where does the truth lie? In England's recent experience has a
growing population been a force for social good or for social
evil? To a considerable extent the level of social welfare depends
on the level of material well-being. In part, then, the influence
that the population variable exerts over the pace of social progress

---

*Among other writers who rejected the idea that population
growth ever brought vice, misery, and poverty in its train see
P. Ravenstone, *A Few Doubts as to the Correctness of some Opinions
Generally Entertained on the Subject of Population and Political
Economy*, London, 1821; G. Poulett Scrope, Principles of Political
Economy, London, 1833; G. K. Rickards, *Population and Capital*,
London, 1854; H. George, *Progress and Poverty*, London, 1884.

is decided by the effect that it has on the pace of economic growth. In the past there have been many occasions when the rate of population increase has outrun the stock of available foodstuffs, and the calamitous economic crises which resulted in such situations, temporarily at least, retarded or even reversed the march of social progress. The disastrous potato famine in Ireland during the 1840s can be regarded as a classic example of the Malthusian nightmare come true, with overpopulation and wretched material conditions generating social misery and disruption of massive proportions.

There have, however, been other societies—and England since the eighteenth century is one—where population has played a very different rôle. Although at times the average material standards of life may have been rather higher if rates of population growth had been a little lower, on balance a growing population in England has contributed positively to the rise in per capita standards of material comfort which became noticeable from the middle of the nineteenth century onwards. Indirectly, therefore, the rapid growth of English population since the Industrial Revolution has helped to create the necessary level of material satisfaction without which real social progress is impossible. *Other things being equal*, people who are well-fed and able to partake of the wide range of consumer goods which a modern economy makes available are likely to be emotionally better balanced, socially more harmonious, and generally more contented with their lot. Moreover, it is only in a relatively flourishing and high-order economy that the mass of the population is able to participate in the increasing range of cultural and recreational pursuits that together help to make life worth living.

But, other things may not be equal. They usually never are. The level of material well-being is by no means the only determinant of social welfare and progress. A society which is becoming better-off in a material sense may, conceivably, be becoming worse-off in other ways. It is possible, indeed, that economic growth itself—the very act of providing people with more of the material things of life—destroys some of the other ingredients necessary to the emergence of a contented, harmonious society. At this point we must look again at some of the other questions posed in the opening sections of this chapter. Has a growing population meant a more vigorous, creative society? Has it produced a more judicious mixture of independence and co-operation among its members? Or, alternatively, has a larger and densely-crowded population been the source of social tension and psychological, psychiatric disorder? Has it, for example, been responsible for the problems of drunkenness, delinquency, crime, suicide and other forms of psychological disturbance which seem to bedevil modern society? To what extent has the growing population been incompatible with the survival of political democracy, with the effective representation of the individual in the political processes? To what extent has it meant the end of any possibility of catering adequately for the needs of the individual or small minority group? Has a large and growing population necessitated the rise of a depersonalised, centralised state bureaucracy in which the 'humanity' of personal contact with the individual, his hopes and his problems has been lost?

As usual in matters of historical demography it is far easier to posit such questions than it is to answer them. The chief difficulty is to find a measurable index (or indices) of individual welfare that relates to the whole period with which we are concerned. For the eighteenth and much of the nineteenth centuries, with certain exceptions, detailed statistical data on the changing patterns of ill-health, crime, suicide, drunkenness and so on— all of them possible indications of the level of individual welfare— are simply not available or, at least, have not yet been thoroughly analysed. Even where such data are available, there are considerable problems involved in using them. A case in point is the evaluation of information on long-term trends in the number of deaths by suicide. As the statistics stand the rate of reported suicide appears to have risen in the course of the nineteenth and twentieth centuries. But it is possible, as Mr Hair points out (*Population Studies*, XXV, 1, 1971), that this increase reflects not so much an actual rise in the incidence of suicide but rather a decrease in the incidence of concealment; that, in other words, in earlier periods fewer suicides were reported. In view of this 'the available evidence leaves it open to doubt whether suicide is more commonly practised today than in the earlier centuries of the modern period'. Similarly, an increase in the absolute and relative number of mental disorders over a given period might merely be a consequence of continuous advances in the standards of psychological and psychiatric medicine, and the recognition of more and more such illnesses where previously they had been overlooked or ignored. By the same token, the apparent increase in criminal activity in England and Wales since the nineteenth century may simply be a statistical illusion, not a reality; the public may have become increasingly more willing to report offences, and the police more willing to act on these reports; the rate of detection may have risen as a result of improvements in methods of policing; or, the apparent rise in criminal activity in recent generations may simply be due to the fact that in the course of economic and social modernisation the range of recognised illegal acts itself widens.

Given such statistical inadequacies, we are forced to admit that as yet no reliable guide to long-term trends in the various indices of individual welfare exists. As they stand at the moment the measurable data which are available have very little real meaning.

We might, however, usefully ask at this point whether English population, at the size, density and rate at which it has grown since the early eighteenth century, could in any case reasonably be expected to have had a serious depressive effect on the level of individual happiness. In the first place there is no evidence to support the belief that a growing population has meant the end of individual political representation or a decrease in society's concern for individual welfare. On the contrary, it cannot be without significance that the nineteenth and twentieth century trends towards a more complete political democracy and a greater concern for individual well-being occurred at precisely the time when the population of England was larger and growing more rapidly than ever before. It may well be that the individual or minority group has a better chance of being heard and of being catered for in a large rather than a small population. Minority groups in small populations may be so tiny that their interests attract little attention. In bigger populations, on the other hand, the size of the minority group may be so large that its needs demand service.

In the second place there is likewise no firm evidence to support the view that the mental stability of modern English society has been seriously upset by high rates of population growth and severe overcrowding. Admittedly recent studies of the effects of overcrowding on the behaviour patterns of rodent populations show that high densities *can* lead to serious mental stress and disturbance (Calhoun, *Scientific American*, 206, 2, 1962). But rodent populations are not human populations; they lack man's ability to adapt himself to changed conditions. And in any case the rate at which the population of England has grown since the eighteenth century has, by comparison with what has since happened in many other parts of the world, been surprisingly moderate. Compared to other societies, the problem of overcrowding has not been unduly severe—certainly not severe enough to have given rise to major crises of mental instability. Moreover, if the psychiatric and psychological health of modern English society has deteriorated (and as we noted previously this still needs to be reliably demonstrated) might not the explanation(s) lie outside the demographic factor? How far, for example, is mental stress the consequence of the greater demands made on the individual by the intense competitiveness of life in a complex, technological world? How far is it due in certain social groups to the modern problem of inactivity and boredom? These and many similar questions will need to be answered before we can properly quantify the contribution of population growth to recent changes in the pattern of mental health.

Nothing in the way of a firm conclusion can be drawn from any of this. Society has long been aware that population may have an influence on the level of individual welfare, through its influence on both physical and mental health. Many writers have seen it as a force for social progress, others as an actual or potential menace to present and future levels of well-being. In the present state of knowledge we cannot with certainty say very much more than this. We do not yet know whether fluctuations in the size and rate of growth of a population have a *significant* influence on trends in the various indices of social welfare; nor are we able to quantify the rôle of population against the part played by other potential determinants of popular happiness and well-being. Least of all can we say whether the demographic factor has been an agent for good or evil. For what a purely subjective view is worth such limited evidence that does exist seems to suggest that, in recent English experience at least, a growing population has on the whole acted as an additional stimulant to the levels of individual welfare—if only because the positive benefits to physical health which stemmed from the contribution made by population increase to economic development have not been outweighed by any obvious association between population growth and deteriorating standards of mental health.

* * *

By way of a postscript to this and previous chapters one last point is worth emphasising. The tentative conclusions that have been presented on the intricate relationship between population, economy and society should be viewed within the context of English experience only. It must not be assumed that the consequences of demographic trends, even in societies where the patterns of population growth are identical to those in England and Wales since the eighteenth century, are everywhere necessarily the same. Population is, after all, only one of the many variables which together shape the direction of economic and social life. And, accordingly, the influence it exerts is in part determined by the extent to which a society is blessed with other essential pre-conditions for economic development. The fact that the rôle of population in England has been generally beneficial owes much to the fortunate coexistence of most of the other requirements for economic growth. In other societies, where the general circumstances are less conducive to economic development, the economic and social consequences of population trends may be very different.

FURTHER READING

Books and Monographs

M. Anderson, *Family Structure in Nineteenth Century Lancashire*, Cambridge University Press, 1971.

J. M. Beshers, *Population Processes in Social Systems*, New York, 1967.

C. Clark, *Population Growth and Land Use*, London, 1967.

E. Durkheim, *The Division of Labour in Society*, New York, 1960.

H. J. Dyos (ed.), *The Study of Urban History*, London, 1968.

D. V. Glass and R. Revelle (eds.), *Population and Social Structure*, London, 1972.

P. M. Hauser, *Population and World Politics*, Glencoe, 1958.

E. M. Hubback, *The Population of Britain*, London, 1947.

R. K. Kelsall, *Population*, London, 1967.

P. Laslett (ed.), *Household and Family in Past Time*, Cambridge University Press, 1972.

P. Laslett, *The World we have Lost*, London, 1965.

D. C. Marsh, *The Changing Social Structure of England and Wales, 1871–1961*, London, revised edition, 1965.

G. Myrdal, *Population. A Problem for Democracy*, Harvard, 1940.

R. Pressat, *Population*, London, 1970.

Royal Commission on Population, *Report*, London H.M.S.O, 1949.

A. Sauvy, *General Theory of Population*, London, 1969.

M. C. Shelesnyak, *Growth of Population, Consequences and Controls*, New York, 1969.

N. J. Smelser, *Social Change in the Industrial Revolution*, London, 1959.

United Nations, *The Determinants and Consequences of Population Trends*, New York, 1953.

United Nations, *The Ageing of Populations and its Economic and Social Implications*, New York, 1956.

E. A. Wrigley (ed.), *An Introduction to English Historical Demography*, London, 1966.

E. A. Wrigley (ed.), *Nineteenth Century Society*, Cambridge University Press, 1972.

Articles

W. A. Armstrong, 'The interpretation of the census books for Victorian towns', in H. J. Dyos (ed.), *The Study of Urban History*, London, 1968.

J. B. Calhoun, 'Population density and social pathology', *Scientific American*, 206, 2, 1962.

G. M. Carstairs, 'Overpopulation and mental health', in H. Reiger and J. Bruce Falls (eds.), *Exploding Humanity: the Crisis of Numbers*, International Forum Foundation, 1969.

K. Davis, 'Demographic foundations of national power', in M. Berger *et al.* (eds.), *Freedom and Control in Modern Society*, New York, 1954.

D. V. Glass, Two papers on Gregory King, in D. V. Glass and D. E. C. Eversley (eds.), *Population in History*, London, 1965.

P. E. Hair, 'A note on the incidence of Tudor suicide', *Local Population Studies*, 5, 1970.

P. E. Hair, 'Deaths from violence in Britain: a tentative secular survey', *Population Studies*, XXV, 1, 1971.

P. Laslett, 'Size and structure of the household in England over three centuries', *Population Studies*, XXIII, 2, 1969.

P. Laslett, 'A comment on J. W. Nixon's note', *Population Studies*, XXIV, 3, 1970.

P. Laslett and J. Harrison, 'Clayworth and Cogenhoe', in H. E. Bell and R. L. Ollard (eds.), *Historical essays, 1600–1750*, London, 1963.

C. M. Law, 'Local censuses in the eighteenth century', *Population Studies*, XXIII, 1, 1969.

R. Lawton, 'The population of Liverpool in the mid-nineteenth century', *Tr. Hist. Soc. Lancs & Chesh*, 107, 1955.

B. A. Liu, 'Population growth and educational development', Annals of the American Academy of Political and Social Science, 371, 1967, reprinted in T. R. Ford and G. F. De Jong (eds.), *Social Demography*, New Jersey, 1970.

J. W. Nixon, 'Comments on Peter Laslett's paper', *Population Studies*, XXIV, 3, 1970.

G. Simmel, 'The significance of numbers for social life', in P. Hare et. al. (eds.), *Small Groups: Studies in Social Interaction*, New York, 1955.

R. Smith, 'Early Victorian household structure', *International Review of Social History*, 15, 1970.

N. L. Tranter, 'Population and social structure in a Bedfordshire parish: the Cardington listing of inhabitants, 1782', *Population Studies*, XXI, 3, 1967.

N. L. Tranter, 'The social structure of a Bedfordshire parish in the mid-nineteenth century: the Cardington census enumerators' books, 1851', *International Review of Social History*, 1973.

H. H. Winsborough, 'The social consequences of high population density', in Ford and De Jong (eds.), op. cit.

Index